JAMES W. LEITCH

The King Comes

An Exposition of Mark 1-7

SCM PRESS LTD
BLOOMSBURY STREET LONDON

FIRST PUBLISHED 1965
© SCM PRESS LTD 1965
PRINTED IN GREAT BRITAIN BY
BILLING AND SONS LTD
GUILDFORD AND LONDON

THE KING COMES

CONTENTS

PREFACE

These expositions were originally a series of sermons. But they have since undergone two changes. In the first instance, further study of Mark's Gospel produced in course of time two new series of sermons on the same texts—in itself surely a testimony to the richness of the Gospel. Secondly, now that they are to be read instead of heard, I have taken advantage of the opportunity to condense and combine all three series into one. As a result, the pieces have acquired a certain hybrid character. They are no longer sermons, for few if any of them could be preached as they now stand. On the other hand, they lack the technical detail to be expected of a scientific exegesis and still bear frequent marks of the spoken word. Perhaps one might call them meditations, or expository reflections.

The old practice of preaching through a book section by section, which is still common on the Continent, has at least two great advantages. It saves the distracting and often frantic search for a text: one knows already at the beginning of the week what next Sunday's text will be, and can concentrate instead on deciding what to say about it. But more important, it also leads the preacher to wrestle with themes he would otherwise have avoided or ignored, and hence to the thrill of new and unexpected discoveries. I hope this book may encourage others to try it for themselves.

The nature of the book's origin explains the omission of names and technicalities, which would have been no help to the original hearers. But it will be obvious that my debts to other writers are many. I would mention especially the sermons of the late Pastor Samuel Dieterle, which inspired me in my student days and were later published with the title *Der Einbruch des Reiches*; but also Professor Austin Farrer's *A Study in St Mark*, and last, but by no means least, Matthew Henry's *An Exposition of the Old and New Testament* (still useful even after 250 years!).

Technical considerations have made it necessary to end the

present volume at 7.37, but I hope a continuation may be possible later.

Basle, February 1965

JAMES W. LEITCH

PROLOGUE

The beginning of the gospel of Jesus Christ, the Son of God; As it is written in the prophets, Behold, I send my messenger before thy face, which shall prepare thy way before thee. The voice of one crying in the wilderness, Prepare ye the way of the Lord, make his paths straight. John did baptize in the wilderness, and preach the baptism of repentance for the remission of sins. And there went out unto him all the land of Judaea, and they of Jerusalem, and were all baptized of him in the river of Jordan, confessing their sins. And John was clothed with camel's hair, and with a girdle of a skin about his loins; and he did eat locusts and wild honey; And preached, saying, There cometh one mightier than I after me, the latchet of whose shoes I am not worthy to stoop down and unloose. I indeed have baptized you with water: but he shall baptize you with the Holy Ghost.

And it came to pass in those days, that Jesus came from Nazareth of Galilee, and was baptized of John in Jordan. And straightway coming up out of the water, he saw the heavens opened, and the Spirit like a dove descending upon him: And there came a voice from heaven, saying, Thou art my beloved Son, in whom I am well pleased. And immediately the Spirit driveth him into the wilderness. And he was there in the wilderness forty days, tempted of Satan; and was with the wild beasts; and the angels ministered unto him. (1.1-13)

It was once the custom among playwrights to begin with a prologue which tells what sort of play is to be presented and what its main themes are to be. The first thirteen verses of Mark's gospel are just such a prologue. What follows is also like a great drama, both in the vividness of the scenes and in the way they are worked together. But it is not by any of the usual names that Mark describes it here. It is neither tragedy nor comedy, not a history, not a morality or miracle play, though it has elements of them all. He calls it *gospel*—'the gospel of Jesus Christ' (1). And 'gospel' is simply another word for 'good news'. No doubt it is well to have a special word for this incomparable good news—*the* Good News of Jesus Christ. But we also do well to remember what the word means. Even the parts of Mark's drama which seem dark with foreboding, or loaded with challenge and warning, are still *good* news. Even the parts that ring strange in modern ears, or appear totally irrelevant to our situation, are still good news *for us*. Whatever the scene before us, we have to understand it as good news, or else we do not understand it at all.

The Good News of Jesus Christ does not come suddenly out of the blue, as news so often does. It begins, says Mark, not with Jesus, but with 'John baptizing in the wilderness and preaching' (4). And even John, he says, comes in fulfilment of a long-standing promise. The prophet Malachi had promised long ago that when God came to renew his world, he would first send a herald and pathbreaker to prepare men for his coming (Mal. 3.1). Isaiah, still longer ago, had spoken of that too (Isa. 40.3). And now, in John, Mark sees these ancient promises fulfilled. He strikes the same note of fulfilment again a few verses later when he describes John as 'clothed with camel's hair, and with a leather girdle about his loins' (6). For then he is surely thinking of the ancient description of Elijah as 'an hairy man, girt with a girdle of leather about his loins' (II Kings 1.8), and of God's promise in the last words of the Old Testament that it would be another Elijah who would be the final herald and pathbreaker (Mal. 4.5 f). When Mark puts these things right in the forefront of his prologue, he means to remind us that the great drama he is going to unfold is one of *fulfilment*: it has its roots firmly in the Old Testament, and again and again it will be in the Old Testament that we shall find the key to many of its scenes.

But to come back to the Baptist: 'The beginning of the Good News of Jesus Christ . . . was John baptizing in the wilderness and preaching the baptism of repentance for the remission of sins' (1, 4). For many that may be only high-sounding religious jargon. And yet it has really quite a simple and straightforward meaning. John's baptism consisted of taking people into the river and washing them there. We do not wash things unless they are dirty and we want them clean. Hence it is called a 'baptism of repentance'—a washing that marks the desire for a new, clean way of life. And we only wash things in the hope that washing will take out the stains. Therefore it is a 'baptism with a view to the remission of sins'—a washing whose purpose is to get rid of the dirt. When John came and set up this baptism in God's name, it was a symbolic act proclaiming God's desire for the cleansing of soiled lives and his intention to cleanse them. When the people came to be baptized at his hands, it was a simple practical way of 'confessing their sins' (5): the very act of offering themselves to be washed was an acknowledgment that they were dirty, and that they wanted cleansing and hoped to receive it.

But at the same time John also insisted that his baptism was only an outward washing with water and what men really needed was thorough cleansing inside as well as out. That was beyond his power to give. But, he said, there was a greater one coming presently—one so much greater that, as John himself put it, 'I am not worthy even to stoop and undo his sandals' (7). And this coming one would not only wash their bodies: he would cleanse them completely in spirit and heart (8). That means that, on John's own showing, his work is only a first step. It is something like the preliminary soaking of the dirty clothes that so often begins the events of washing-day. Everyone knows that for washday itself far greater strength and endurance is needed than for merely steeping in water. But when we see things being put to steep, we know that the work of washing-day is already beginning. That is the really significant thing about John. His work, as he himself interprets it, is a sort of initial steeping of soiled humanity as a visible token both of God's will to cleanse and of the recipients' desire for cleansing. It proclaims the beginning of the great day of Good News. It proclaims also that the best and greatest part is still to come.

And now, almost as if John's words were hardly out of his mouth when the one he spoke of came, Mark presses on at once to tell of his coming and to announce the three great recurring themes that form the heart of the Good News itself.

The first of these is the manner of his coming: 'It came to pass in those days, that Jesus came from Nazareth of Galilee, and was baptized of John in Jordan' (9). What is he doing there, this one who was so great that John (to paraphrase his own words) was not even good enough to lick his boots? What is *he* doing, stooping beneath John among the conscience-stricken crowds who longed for help? The answer is very simple—and very wonderful. If you want to help a drowning man, there are various things you can do. You can stand and shout instructions from the bank. You can throw a rope and hope he will be able to catch it and hang on. But if you want to be sure of helping him, you will dive in beside him and get your arms round him and *bring* him out. And that is

what is happening here. Jesus deliberately making himself one
with these crowds in their desperate need—that is our guarantee
right at the start that no man is too dirty, none too low, none too
lost for Christ. He never leaves us alone, never fobs us off with
good advice, never merely lets down a lifeline in the form of
inspiration or ideals. Whatever and wherever we are, he comes
right down beside us and takes hold of us, in order to be quite
sure of getting us out alive. That in itself is surely good news.

But there is also the second of Mark's great themes: 'And
straightway coming up out of the water, he saw the heavens
opened, and the Spirit like a dove descending upon him: And
there came a voice from heaven, saying, Thou art my beloved
Son, in whom I am well pleased' (10-11). However we may like to
picture that experience, one thing at least is clear: it is Jesus'
assurance that in all he does he has God's authority and God's
approval. And it is surely in order to give us the same assurance
that it is recounted here. It is good to know that in every condition
Christ is right beside us and ready to help. But it will be small
comfort after all unless we know that he is also *able* to give *real*
help. And if his coming to baptism proclaims the one, then the
vision and voice that follow proclaim the other. This would-be
rescuer is not like the weak swimmer who nobly dives to the help
of a drowning man with little chance of doing anything other
than drown along with him. This is the Son of God, endowed with
the whole Spirit and power of God, and therefore certain to succeed in the task he has chosen. Not only so, but as if to make
assurance doubly sure, Mark makes clear that it is not, if one may
put it so, merely a bright idea on Jesus' part that he should come
to our rescue like this: it is a definite part of God's own plan,
and God himself is 'well pleased' that he should set about it as he
does. That he comes thus with the authority, the Spirit and the
commission *of God*—that is good news indeed.

The third of Mark's great themes is this: 'And immediately the
Spirit driveth him into the wilderness, and he was there in the
wilderness forty days, tempted of Satan; and was with the wild
beasts; and the angels ministered unto him' (12-13). At first sight
there is something perplexing, not to say disappointing about that.
For we should rather have expected that one so divinely endowed
would go on at once from triumph to triumph until everyone lived
happily ever after. And yet, that would in fact be a stupid thing to
expect. For this is not a tale of fairy godmothers, but a drama of

real life, and there things do not work out so simply. Real life has been so ordered that living it is always a costly business. And Christ would not really have been one with us after all if he had been spared the cost. To go to the rescue of a drowning man is at once to be exposed to all the dangers to which he is exposed. And so it is also with Jesus. The Spirit which drove him to start by taking his place beside us thereby inevitably drives him into the teeth of the powers that threaten our destruction. What we are shown here is the start of what was to be a constant and costly conflict. But its many different phases can be reduced to one fundamental issue. And that issue is subtly stated by the very voice that greeted Jesus as he came up from Jordan. For 'Thou art my Son' is a quotation from the Old Testament addressed to the glorious King who would rule the nations with a rod of iron and crush all opposition out of hand (Ps. 2.7 f); but 'the beloved in whom I am well pleased' was God's description of a very different Old Testament figure—the suffering servant who would not advertise himself, but with great gentleness and patience would establish an order of justice and truth (Isa. 42.1 ff). Which now was to be Jesus' way?—the way of self-assertion or of self-sacrifice? the way of show or of quiet perseverance? the way of domination or of service? He must have seen clearly enough that the second way was the only true one, and no doubt it was the strength of God, or what Mark here calls the presence of the angels, that enabled him to choose it. But there can be just as little doubt that he must have felt the attraction of the other as keenly as we all do. And not all the angels in heaven, nor even God himself, could spare him the cost of taking the way he did. The forty days' struggle alone among the beasts of the wilderness is only a shadow and foretaste of what that cost was going to be. It stands here in Mark's prologue to tell us at the outset that our rescue is a costly business, and that he is ready to pay the price.

These themes will be elaborated in the scenes that follow. But here already we have, in briefest outline, the Good News of Jesus Christ the long-promised Rescuer of men: he has come to be one with all whose lives are in danger, and will not stop short of even the lowest. He has come as God's own Son, with God's Spirit in him and the full authority of God behind him, so that literally nothing can thwart him in the work of rescue. And though that work be long and often bitter, he will spare no cost in order to complete it.

But this is not just an ancient story: it is still good news for today. And it is not only for men in general that he came: he still comes like that for us. It all began, Mark says, with John baptizing and preaching and men coming to listen and be baptized—and even as that was happening, Jesus was on his way. It begins that way still. With a man commissioned by God to baptize with water and to preach. With men who are willing to be baptized and to listen to his witness because they recognize, however vaguely, that there is something wrong with them and long for better. And even while we speak, Christ himself is near, to do what neither water nor sermon, neither preacher nor congregation could ever do. That is why it can all so easily begin again for us.

ACT I

The King in Action

SCENE 1: *WORK AND WORSHIP*

Now after that John was put in prison, Jesus came into Galilee, preaching the gospel of the kingdom of God, And saying, The time is fulfilled, and the kingdom of God is at hand: repent ye, and believe the gospel.

Now as he walked by the sea of Galilee, he saw Simon and Andrew his brother casting a net into the sea: for they were fishers. And Jesus said unto them, Come ye after me, and I will make you to become fishers of men. And straightway they forsook their nets, and followed him. And when he had gone a little farther thence, he saw James the son of Zebedee, and John his brother, who also were in the ship mending their nets. And straightway he called them: and they left their father Zebedee in the ship with the hired servants, and went after him.

And they went into Capernaum; and straightway on the sabbath day he entered into the synagogue, and taught. And they were astonished at his doctrine: for he taught them as one that had authority, and not as the scribes.

And there was in their synagogue a man with an unclean spirit; and he cried out, Saying, Let us alone; what have we to do with thee, thou Jesus of Nazareth? art thou come to destroy us? I know thee who thou art, the Holy One of God. And Jesus rebuked him, saying, hold thy peace, and come out of him. And when the unclean spirit had torn him, and cried with a loud voice, he came out of him. And they were all amazed, insomuch that they questioned among themselves, saying, What thing is this? what new doctrine is this? for with authority commandeth he even the unclean spirits, and they do obey him. And immediately his fame spread abroad throughout all the region round about Galilee. (1.14-28)

'The time is fulfilled, and the kingdom of God is at hand: repent ye, and believe the gospel' (15). That was the tremendous message with which Jesus now burst upon his contemporaries. And what an effect it had! Four tough working men left their jobs on the spot. A respectable city congregation was thoroughly shaken up. And one man, after creating a most extraordinary scene, found such peace of mind as he had never known. The same sort of thing could happen still, if we would only grasp what the message means.

'The time is up.' The time of waiting and groping, when it was 'each man for himself and the devil take the hindmost'. And yet men could not simply follow their own bent unrestrained. They had to live together in some sort of order. So they had to discover rules by which to order their common life. Some of these were given the authority of divine commands or a universal moral code, while others were mere conventions, like the rules of 'polite society' or the changing laws of circumstance. But behind it all, at bottom it was still each man for himself, and a constant struggle to keep your end up and not be done down by the next man. We know that order very well, for it is the order in which we all try to live. We know its bright side and its dark side, its thrills and joys and triumphs, its frustrations, its temptations, its constant fears. But Jesus knows it better still. And he tells us its time is up. It is finished and has no more point. True, it still lingers on somehow, strangely, all too obviously. But it lingers like a flower cut from its roots. It may look imposing, even attractive. But there is no real life in it, no real strength, and presently it will wither and disappear.

The old order's time is up, because now Christ is here and with him the new order, the kingdom of God, is already breaking in all round us. Because in Christ God is with us and for us and claims us all for himself. He has come to bring a new régime in which it is no longer each man for himself and the devil take the hindmost, but instead each man for God, and God for us all, and the devil is left lamenting. A new order where we are not given rules to observe, but a Person to follow and love. A new brotherhood in which fear and suspicion of each other are swallowed up in common allegiance to him. With the coming of Christ such things are no longer a pious dream: they are already living reality, right at hand, at our very door.

That is the first thing he wants us now to hear. But he wants us to hear it not only with ears and heads but also with our hearts. And so the second part of his message is a call to 'repent and believe this Good News'.

We are apt to shy at that word 'repentance' because of the

weird associations it has come to have. But first and foremost it means simply a change of purpose and direction, a change of heart. What Jesus asks of us here is to stop being so tied to the old order and its ways, to begin taking our direction and purpose from God, to set our hearts on him instead of ourselves. And is that not the only thing to do, if the time is up, as he says? As long as a game lasts, there is some point in observing its rules. But once the whistle has gone, men turn their attention to other things. Anyone who stayed on, trying to get more points or goals, would only look ridiculous. But we are making ourselves just as ridiculous if, now that Christ is here and, so to speak, the whistle has gone, we insist on keeping to our old ways and rules and seeking our own ends.

A lot depends, of course, on whether we believe the whistle really has gone. So many people seem to be carrying on as if it had not, and the game still seems so very real. But it is facts that count, and appearances can never alter the facts. I may look the picture of health and feel perfectly well. But if the doctor in charge of the mass X-ray unit tells me that there is in fact a shadow on my lung, then I should be signing my own death-warrant if I refused to believe him. It is much the same with Jesus. He is like the doctor who sees deeper than we can see. If *he* tells us that the old order's time is up, then we should be extremely foolish not to take his word for it, whatever the appearances. We shall be missing all the best things in life—we shall be missing life itself—if we do not join the ever-growing company of those who believe him and take their places under the new régime.

But the next verses show us at once that Jesus is much more than a preacher. He does not merely tell men about the new order, and leave the rest to them. He comes right into their lives to bring them into it. And where he starts is in their everyday, working lives. Two men at their daily work, 'casting a net into the sea, for they were fishers' (16). But this is no time for merely making a livelihood: 'Come on, follow me, and I will make you fishers of men' (17). And off they go without more ado. The next pair he sees are mending their nets. Mending mere nets, when there are so many broken hearts and broken lives to mend! So he calls them too, 'and they left their father with the labourers, and went after him' (20). Never mind whether they abandoned their jobs for good and all. (They seem to have kept their boat, anyway, and we hear of them fishing again.) The chief point is surely: they had found a new orientation and purpose for their working life. It was no longer their own private concern, no longer just to keep body and soul together with perhaps a bit over for the odd comfort. Now they worked as disciples of Christ, and whatever they did, he could use it to win men for his kingdom.

He still seeks to bring the same transformation into *our* working lives. It is not a question of what sort of work we do, but of our attitude to it. For many the main thing is how much they can make and how high they can climb. For others work is a necessary evil, which has to be put up with in order to have the where-withal to live. For some it has become an end in itself, so that they live for their work and would be entirely lost without it. These are some of the commonest attitudes. But they are the attitudes of the old order—futile and antiquated. In Christ's new order, and for all who believe in it, our daily work has a far deeper and richer meaning. Whether it be congenial or uncongenial, whether it be in an office or factory or shop, in a home, in a school, or wherever else it may be—it was given us in order to provide particular contacts with other people, special openings through which Christ's influence can be brought to bear on them. And the really important thing is not the size of the weekly pay packet or the annual bank balance, not even the amount of satisfaction we find in our work. What matters most is: how many men and women are won through it for Christ.

So much for our workaday lives. From work Jesus now goes on to worship: 'They went into Capernaum; and straightway on the sabbath day he entered into the synagogue, and taught' (21). There, too, he turned everything upside down. They were accustomed to endless, sleepy rigmaroles, with now and then perhaps a clever, polished address—but at bottom always the same old stereotyped opinions. But this was different. Here was someone who did not quote the recognized authorities, but made himself an Authority. He did not go in for the usual, 'Rabbi so-and-so has said this, and the church teaches that': he said, 'Verily *I* say unto you . . .', and his words were alive and compelling. Mark says the hearers were 'astonished' (22), which in his language is a very strong word. It does not mean merely that they were greatly surprised. It means they were shaken to the depths of their being.

The strange thing is, that so often we still live as if it all never happened, or at least would never happen again. We may go to church for many reasons—habit, respectability, a sense of duty, or because we feel the need of a moral tonic or a spiritual sedative. And there we listen (or it may be, pretend to listen) to a 'sermon' on some religious topic. It may all be dreadfully dull. It may also be very pleasant, even stirring. And yet, how frightfully out of date! For it is centuries since all that was shown to be beside the point. In Christ's new order, and for all who believe in it, worship means meeting together with *him*, hearing what *he* has to say to us. We do not have to make any secret of our preachers' fallibility and our own spiritual deafness. But we know that still, when Sunday comes Christ goes into the church and teaches—now no longer limited to one particular church as in the days of his earthly life. We gather here with expectation, because we believe he can and will take up the preacher's stumbling words into his service and enable us to hear through them his own word to us. And when that happens, then we are no longer left with mere opinions which we can listen to or ignore as we please (because of course opinions vary, and one man's are as good as another's, and anyway we have heard it all before). When *Christ* speaks to us, he tells us the truth about our lives—truth that goes home, truth that commits. When Christ goes into the church and teaches, then worship becomes a living, breath-taking experience.

These are two of the amazing things that happen under his new régime: he comes to rescue our work from the domination of self-interest, and to deliver our worship from the curse of mediocrity. Only, let us beware of oversimplifying. Not everyone is swept into the new order as easily as the four Galilean fishermen, or so quickly thrilled as the congregation in Capernaum. For there is no reason why everything should go like clockwork the moment Christ appears. We have likened him to the rescuer of a drowning man. But it often happens that the drowning man in his panic attacks his rescuer. And now Mark shows us that that can happen with Jesus too: there was a man there who panicked and turned on him screaming, 'Leave us in peace and go and mind your own business! Have you come here to destroy us? I know who you are—God's Holy One' (24).

It was a man 'with an unclean spirit' (23), which is the biblical way of saying he was mad. But it seems that with the often uncanny insight of the mentally deranged he saw at once what was happening here. He saw that this was the 'Holy One of God', whose presence men can so ill abide. He saw the enormity of what Jesus was asking—literally all or nothing—and the frightful risk of staking everything on him. He saw enough, at least, to fear for his life. And surely he had reason to be afraid. For he must have known what Mark mentions at the beginning of this scene as if it were a matter of common knowledge: that even as Jesus was speaking of the new régime, John who had served as its herald was languishing in gaol. He must have seen standing there beside Jesus the four men whose unthinking obedience to his summons had left them now without any visible means of support. He could not know how John's imprisonment was going to end, or what trials lay in store for the four disciples. But he could make a shrewd enough guess to rebel against becoming personally involved: 'Have you come to destroy us? Go and leave us in peace!'

Perhaps none but a madman would have made such a scene about it. And yet, surely he was saying what many of the rest must also have been thinking and only he was fool enough to blurt out—what many of us, too, must have been thinking if we have really been listening to Christ now. For is there not the same 'unclean spirit' in us all—the unclean spirit of Self? As long as we can succeed in regarding Christ as one who comforts and helps and strengthens and inspires, one who will enable us to live our lives as we should like them to be—as long as we can believe he will look after our interests, or at least what will prove in the end to be our true interests—then we shall be ready to welcome him to a place, perhaps a very high place, among our allegiances. But when our worship becomes alive and we find ourselves face to face with Christ as the Lord who claims *sole* authority over us— then there is something in us that rebels, then the unclean spirit of self-interest cries out against him. How can we commit ourselves to him alone? How can we turn our back on our comforts and needs, our plans and hopes and noble aspirations and all the other things on which we build our lives? He seems to threaten the whole foundation of our living and thinking. He seems to be asking us to let go everything we know and understand, and leap into the dark. And that is such an appalling prospect that it is small wonder if we feel like sending him about his business because we would rather be left in peace.

It is of course madness. It is preferring the peace of death to the struggle that is life, just because we have no guarantee that it really is life. But it is a promising kind of madness after all. It is at least far more promising than indifference or pretence. For it is playing right into Christ's hands—because he is only too pleased to mind his own business, because his business is precisely with the unclean spirits that mar our lives. He is indeed God's Holy One— the one specially set apart by God to free us from them. In that Jewish synagogue he took up the challenge at once, with startling results: one last convulsion, a final scream—and suddenly the man was sitting quietly at his feet. Don't let us make the mistake of wanting to know how it happened. The point is, that somehow or other it did happen and it stands here as our promise that it can happen again. Christ can still 'command even unclean spirits' (27), and still they must obey his command. Today he is ready to do the same for us as he did before—to cast out that ugly, rebellious spirit of Self, and give us instead the free, joyful spirit of those who are wholly committed to him. He can. One way or another— suddenly or slowly, startlingly or imperceptibly—he will. Then we, too, shall discover the thrill of working and worshipping under his new régime. Then we, too, shall see to it that once more 'his fame spreads abroad throughout all the region round about' (28).

SCENE 2: *SICKNESS AND SUFFERING*

And forthwith, when they were come out of the synagogue, they entered into the house of Simon and Andrew, with James and John. But Simon's wife's mother lay sick of a fever, and anon they tell him of her. And he came and took her by the hand, and lifted her up; and immediately the fever left her, and she ministered unto them.

And at even, when the sun did set, they brought unto him all that were diseased, and them that were possessed with devils. And all the city was gathered together at the door. And he healed many that were sick of divers diseases, and cast out many devils; and suffered not the devils to speak, because they knew him.

And in the morning, rising up a great while before day, he went out, and departed into a solitary place, and there prayed. And Simon and they that were with him followed after him. And when they had found him, they said unto him, All men seek for thee. And he said unto them, Let us go into the next towns, that I may preach there also: for therefore came I forth. And he preached in their synagogues throughout all Galilee, and cast out devils.

And there came a leper to him, beseeching him, and kneeling down to him, and saying unto him, If thou wilt, thou canst make me clean. And Jesus, moved with compassion, put forth his hand, and touched him, and saith unto him, I will; be thou clean. And as soon as he had spoken, immediately the leprosy departed from him, and he was cleansed. And he straitly charged him, and forthwith sent him away; And saith unto him, See thou say nothing to any man: but go thy way, shew thyself to the priest, and offer for thy cleansing those things which Moses commanded, for a testimony unto them. But he went out, and began to publish it much, and to blaze abroad the matter, insomuch that Jesus could no more openly enter into the city, but was without in desert places: and they came to him from every quarter. (1.29-45)

Jesus did not only take his new disciples to church to hear his preaching. He also went straight home with them after the service to share their lunch and spend the rest of the day. And there at Simon's house he began to do some more of the extraordinary things that happened wherever he went.

The story begins normally enough. It was only natural that they should excuse the absence of Simon's mother-in-law, who should have been the hostess but was in bed with a feverish chill. It was natural, too, that Jesus should presently go to see her. But then the extraordinary thing happened. Instead of the usual remarks about being sorry and hoping she would soon be better, Jesus 'took her by the hand, and lifted her up; and immediately the fever left her' (31)—left her, too, not washed out as everyone is after a sharp bout of 'flu', but as ready and able to look after her guests as if she had never been ill at all. When a thing like that happens in a small town, you do not wonder that word of it spreads like wildfire. You do not wonder either that as soon as the Sabbath was over and it was permissible to carry invalids about, all the physical and mental wrecks were brought to him and the whole population seemed to be massed at that one cottage door. But then the extraordinary thing happens again: 'He healed many that were sick of various diseases, and cast out many devils; and suffered not the devils to speak, because they knew him' (34).

We cannot take in the scene. Even our imagination staggers at it. But one thing stands out perfectly clear. And that is, that Jesus is no advocate of the 'pie in the sky when you die' type of Christianity. He does not put these wretched creatures off by telling them it will all come right in the end, and meantime they must

simply thole their sufferings as best they can: he sets about healing and helping them at once. Surely he could not have made it
plainer that sickness and suffering are enemies and intruders in
God's world. In the new order which Christ brings, they are not to
be put up with: they are to be attacked and triumphed over.

That is something that should be made known in every hospital
and sickroom and laboratory, and in every distressed area large or
small. Here is endless inspiration for doctors and nurses and all
who are engaged in the struggle against disease, for social and
welfare workers too, and also for every sufferer who refuses to let
his troubles get him down. We are not merely left to ourselves to
battle on grimly and hope for the best. We are called to take our
place here and now in Christ's new order, where all *his* resources
are available to heal and save.

That in itself is something quite tremendous. But the next verses
of our text go on to tell us another striking thing which is equally
important. It must have been a long and exhausting evening, but
for all that Jesus 'rising up a great while before day, went out, and
departed into a solitary place, and there prayed' (35). It is tempt-
ing to draw a moral from that about the importance of prayer.
And true enough, if it is in the name of Christ that we seek to
triumph over suffering, then we shall find prayer so important that
we shall make time for it, even at the cost of 'getting up a great
while before day'. But that is not the really striking thing here.
When the gospels tell us of Jesus praying, it is always when he is
faced by a great temptation or a great decision. And this occasion
is clearly no exception. We are not told what he prayed about, but
we are told enough about the result to be able to guess. Apparently Jesus did not by any means share the general delight at the
success of the last evening's work. He found it a new temptation—
or rather an old one in a new dress. 'If you are the Christ,' the
tempter had said before, 'give them bread from stones, and they
will all follow you.' 'If you are the Christ,' he was saying now,
'cure their troubles, and you will have them all.' But Jesus was not
a humane Healer with a patent cure for every ill. He had come
from God to win men back to God. In face of the temptation he
turns again to his Father. And there he makes his decision again:
man does not live by health alone any more than by bread
alone. It is by the word of God that men live, and without that
nothing else is any use at all. It would be too easy to fill their

stomachs and heal their pains. For it was what they all wanted, and what his own compassion must have urged him to do. It would be costly—terribly costly—to bring them God's word and win them to accept it. For they were not so interested in that, and he knew it well. But at all costs it must be done. That is why, when the disciples came racing after him and wanted to drag him back to carry on the good work, he refused: 'Let us go into the next towns, that I may *preach* there also: for that is what I came for' (38).

It must have been a blow to the disciples' enthusiasm, and it should pull us up sharply too. But it most emphatically does *not* mean that what we said a moment ago about triumphing over suffering here and now was all a mistake, and we have to go back to the 'pie in the sky when you die' after all. The healings were no mistake, and they did not stop there. For the very next verse says, 'He preached in their synagogues throughout all Galilee, *and cast out devils*' (39). And the rest of our text tells how he went on to cure a leper as well. So the mastery of suffering still has its place. But here it is put in its *proper* place. It is still important, and we should never forget how important it is. But, says Jesus, the preaching is more important still. To our way of thinking that seems strange. For we want above all to be practical. The great cry today is not for more sermons, but for more action. That is understandable enough. And it is largely the church's own fault, because too often her message has been dull and uninspiring. But the remedy is not to abandon preaching and concentrate on doing things. It is to rediscover a message that is really Good News. To say, 'It is not sermons but deeds that count', is as if a man should say, 'It is the plumbing that counts, not the reservoir'. And then he goes and builds a house with the finest system of waterpipes and drains and all the most modern sanitary installations. But in the end it is useless: there is no water, because he has not troubled about a connection to the reservoir and the water-main. So, too, we may build the finest system of hospitals and welfare services. But they can be no real blessing unless they are constantly supplied by the healing streams that flow down from God through the preaching of the Gospel. Only God's love can inspire lasting enthusiasm for the work of healing. Only he can direct and correct our zeal. Unless he is known and his sovereignty taken seriously, everything else is bound to go wrong. We are certainly called to take our place in the offensive against suffering. Here we are also called—still more urgently—to do it as those whose inspiration and direction comes from God.

The story of the leper repeats these two points, and adds a third. Here is a man who comes to Jesus, 'beseeching him, and kneeling down to him, and saying unto him, If thou wilt, thou canst make me clean' (40). Here again Jesus' response is immediate practical help: 'He put forth his hand, and touched him, and saith unto him, I will; be thou clean. And as soon as he had spoken, immediately the leprosy departed from him, and he was cleansed' (41-2). But here again is the note of dissatisfaction. Our text says that Jesus was 'moved with compassion' (41), but it seems most likely that what Mark actually wrote was 'moved with *anger*'. Various reasons have been suggested for that. But after all we have said, surely what annoyed him was just that here was another man running after him for a cure, as if that were all that mattered. He does not stop to read the poor man a lecture. He heals first and rebukes afterwards. But the rebuke is there just the same: 'He sternly charged him, and forthwith sent him away; and saith unto him, See thou say nothing to any man: but go thy way, show thyself to the priest, and offer for thy cleansing those things which Moses commanded, for a testimony unto them' (43-4). In other words, the man was not to imagine that he was now free to go off and do what he liked with his new-found health. The Law laid down certain things that a cleansed leper had to do. He could not have done them before, even if he had wanted to. But now that he was cured he was able at last to obey the Law. And at once Jesus sternly charges him to remember that and do it. Unfortunately he did not. He put publicity before obedience, and went off to make his story headline news. And it was Jesus who had to suffer for it: he was forced out into the desert again—this time not alone with the devil, but surrounded by masses of people who were now as eager as the devil had been to get him to perform miracles instead of carrying on with his real task.

Here we can see the third important thing about Christ's healing power. We have already seen that he offers it not just in the dim and distant future, but here and now. We have also seen that his healing has its source not just in humane sympathies but in the **heart of God**, and everything goes wrong when we try to separate it from the message of God's kingdom. Now we have to learn that he heals with a definite purpose. And the purpose is, that men should be the better able to serve God. Christ did not come to found a super Welfare State in which there would be no more headaches or nerves or diseases and men could enjoy life without bothering about God. That would appeal to many, and would suit us all very well. But the new order Christ came to found is one in which God is supreme and men find their happiness in serving him. He will enable us to master our troubles. He will help us over everything that distracts us and hinders our service. But once he has done his part, ours is to obey. His blessings are not to be used for our own enjoyment in our own way. We are meant to use them for the service of God in whatever way he asks. Otherwise we only make nuisances of ourselves as the leper did.

SCENE 3: *SIN*

And again he entered into Capernaum after some days; and it was noised that he was in the house. And straightway many were gathered together, insomuch that there was no room to receive them, no, not so much as about the door: and he preached the word unto them. And they come unto him, bringing one sick of the palsy, which was borne of four. And when they could not come nigh unto him for the press, they uncovered the roof where he was: and when they had broken it up, they let down the bed wherein the sick of the palsy lay. When Jesus saw their faith, he said unto the sick of the palsy, Son, thy sins be forgiven thee. But there were certain of the scribes sitting there, and reasoning in their hearts, Why doth this man thus speak blasphemies? who can forgive sins but God only? And immediately when Jesus perceived in his spirit that they so reasoned within themselves, he said unto them, Why reason ye these things in your hearts? Whether is it easier to say to the sick of the palsy, Thy sins be forgiven thee; or to say, Arise, and take up thy bed, and walk? But that ye may know that the Son of man hath power on earth to forgive sins, (he saith to the sick of the palsy,) I say unto thee, Arise, and take up thy bed, and go thy way into thine house. And immediately he arose, took up the bed, and went forth before them all; insomuch that they were all amazed, and glorified God, saying, We never saw it on this fashion. (2.1-12)

So now Jesus was back in Capernaum again. He had left it because things were beginning to go wrong—because they were so set on cures that they had no ears for his message, and did not really seem to care about him at all except for what they could get out of him. But he had not left them for good. He was not going to give them up as easily as that. He allowed a few days for the excitement to die down. And then he was back again to give them another chance. As soon as word got round, they were after him again, till the house was packed to overflowing. And this time they seemed to be in a better frame of mind, more ready to listen. For we are told that he was able to 'preach the word to them' (2).

But it was not to be for long. Soon he was interrupted by five men, one of them paralysed and carried by the other four; and when they could not get through the crowd, they adopted the extraordinary plan of digging through the roof above his head and lowering the paralytic down through it. It must have been a noisy interruption, for even eastern roofs are not so easily broken up. It may well have been an unwelcome one, too, for it looked like the old business of 'cures at any cost' all over again. But Jesus apparently took it as the sign of a faith so sure of his saving power that it would go to any lengths to get to him. And he was always ready to respond to a faith like that. 'When Jesus saw their faith, he said to the paralytic'—what an anticlimax!—he only said, 'Son, thy sins be forgiven thee' (5).

You can almost see their faces fall! Was he going to lecture the poor creature about his sins instead of doing something about his obvious desperate need? That was what the Pharisees might have done, with their idea that sickness was the direct result of sin, and a punishment for it. It is the sort of thing the church has often been accused of doing—talking as if men's souls were so important that their bodies do not really matter. But it was not Jesus' way. He seems in fact, judging by Mark's portrait, to have been reluctant to mention 'sins' at all. For it is only now that we hear the word on his lips for the first time, and he never uses it again but once (3.28)—which, incidentally, is a striking thing, considering how many of his later followers never seem to tire of it! He is normally much less hesitant in coming to grips with sickness and suffering, branding them as intruders in God's kingdom, and declaring war on them in no uncertain terms. If he appears to hesitate now, then surely it is in another attempt to keep the business of healing in its proper perspective. He had tried to do that for the leper by impressing on him that he had not been freed from his plague just in order to please himself, but so that he could serve God better; and in token of that he was to go to the temple and bring the proper thank-offerings of a cleansed leper. But it had not worked. The man had disobeyed, and only made things more difficult for him. So he tried a different method this time. Perhaps if he put first things first, they would begin to understand. Paralysis is certainly a very horrible thing. But the first and greatest affliction of all is the sins that poison and destroy our relation to God and separate us from him. That is worse even than any paralysis, because paralysis means hampered life, but separation from God means *death*. And not all the health and strength in the world can help us unless our relation to God is set in order. Perhaps if he laid his finger on that first, dealt with that great invisible affliction before attending to the more obvious bodily one—perhaps then they would begin to grasp what he was after. So his first word was: 'Son, thy sins are forgiven thee.'

But still they did not understand. They only started muttering that there was something wrong here, that only God could forgive sins and so this man was obviously talking blasphemy. They *might* have come to a different conclusion. They might have said: 'Only God can forgive sins, and now this new prophet is doing it, so he must be more than a prophet.' But they were far too prejudiced and narrow-minded for such a thought ever to occur to them. And after all, anybody could say what Jesus was saying, and it made no difference—none that you could see, anyway, for the man was still as paralysed as ever and everything looked the same as it had always been. But Jesus understood their difficulty, and did his best to help them. He knew how attached we mortals are to things we can see and feel and 'prove'. So he offered them a sign that they *could* see. It was just as easy to say, 'Arise, take up your mat and walk' as to say, 'Your sins are forgiven' (9). And if they saw the man cured at his word, then surely they could believe sins were forgiven when he said so. 'That you may know that the Son of man has power on earth to forgive sins . . . I say to you, Arise, take up your mat and go home' (10-11). And there it was. 'Immediately he arose, took up the mat and went forth before them all' (12).

Did they *now* understand? We are told that 'they were all amazed, and glorified God, saying, We never saw the like of this before' (12). That does not look very like proper understanding. It looks more like a burst of terrific excitement mixed with superstition. But the main thing is that *we* should understand. So let us go through the story again, and see if we cannot grasp something of the promise it contains for us.

So often, like these people of Capernaum, we have misunderstood Christ and his message, or only half understood. But he has come again to give us another chance. And now, like the paralytic, we lie at his feet. Some have been brought by friends, others were once brought and have somehow lingered on, all are the victims of particular aches and pains, weaknesses and failings, nerves and worries and fears and a whole host of other things that cramp and paralyse us and prevent us from enjoying life. We do not need to count them all up. For he knows them all as well as we do—and better. But he looks for something else—for our faith, our confidence in his power to help. And when he sees that, he always responds—though not always quite in the way we might expect.

Today he lays his finger first of all on our *sins*—our individual share in men's common rebellion against God and all the big and little sins we add to it a thousand times a day. Perhaps we shall understand this better, if we begin by reflecting for a moment on what happens when we start the day by getting up on the wrong side of our bed. We are grumpy and jumpy and difficult. We take ourselves far too seriously. And just nothing seems to go right. Even when people try to be nice to us, we purposely get them wrong. We may know quite well we are making ourselves impossible. But somehow it is so difficult to snap out of it, and whatever we do only seems to make things worse. It is something like that with these sins of ours that come between us and God. We get off on the wrong foot with him from the start, and then nothing goes right. We take ourselves so seriously, and behave like thoroughly spoilt children, and even misuse his kindnesses until they make us more discontented than ever. We have been at it so long that it has become almost a 'second nature' to us and we may never realize how impossible we are making ourselves. But even if we do—even if we begin to wonder how God puts up with us, and recognize that he can hardly be expected to go on for ever—there still seems to be nothing we can do to get back on a right footing with him. But now Christ has come to do something about it. He comes to tell us that our sins are forgiven—all of them from the greatest to the least. They are taken away. They do not count any more. God is now with us—*for* us—and who or what can then be against us?

That is his first word to us today. And it is a tremendous word. But it is not his only one. He knows us too well for that. He knows how much we need some tangible token of his forgiveness and his favour, if we are to be really sure of them. He knows, too, that forgiveness for the past will not help us very much unless he also gives us the strength to go on from here. So now his second word sets us alongside the forgiven cripple who suddenly found himself carrying that mat which had carried him so long, going off to take an active part in the life of that home where he had so long been a burden. Now that Jesus has dealt with our sins, he turns his attention to those weaknesses of body and mind and character of which we are so much more aware—he turns to them and says, 'Arise, take up your mat, and go home.'

What more could we want than that? And yet there *is* more. For we can see in this story a promise that is not just for today or tomorrow or next week. There is promise here also for the grim day when the last great paralysis comes over us, when we are carried out by our friends, and they dig a hole, and let down the coffin in which we lie. . . . An ugly picture, and a morbid one? Surely not, when you see it in the light of our text. For then, like the cripple of old, we shall lie at Jesus' feet. Then only one thing will count—not our achievements, not our position, not even our goodness. He will look only for *faith*—ours and our friends'. And when he sees that, he will say for the last time, 'Son, daughter, thy sins are forgiven thee. . . . Arise—and go *home*.'

Scene 4: *BARRIERS*

And he went forth again by the sea side; and all the multitude resorted unto him, and he taught them. And as he passed by, he saw Levi the son of Alphaeus sitting at the receipt of custom, and said unto him, Follow me. And he arose and followed him. And it came to pass, that, as Jesus sat at meat in his house, many publicans and sinners sat also together with Jesus and his disciples: for there were many, and they followed him. And when the scribes and Pharisees saw him eat with publicans and sinners, they said unto his disciples, How is it that he eateth and drinketh with publicans and sinners? When Jesus heard it, he saith unto them, They that are whole have no need of the physician, but they that are sick: I came not to call the righteous, but sinners to repentance. (2.13-17)

Jesus makes nonsense of the wedge we try to drive between religion and life. He takes the lakeside as seriously as the synagogue. He comes to transform our worship. But he is equally interested in our work, our sufferings, our sins—everything, in fact, that goes on in the hurly-burly of life. And he pays just as little respect to the other wedge we try to drive between the select few and the common mob, between the respectable West End and the rest of the population. He concerns himself with the whole of life, but also with everyone who has to do with it: 'He went forth again by the sea side; and all the multitude resorted unto him, and he taught them' (13).

In the story that follows we see him crossing another well-known barrier—the one that separates the upright and the disreputable, the earnest and the lax. He was not satisfied with teaching the eager masses and helping those who believed in his power. He seeks out also the careless and the indifferent. He sees one man quite unconcerned by what is going on, and busy making money in his own unpleasant way—a man who has no interest in Jesus, unless he should want to cross the frontier and have something to declare, in which case there will be customs duty to collect, plus the usual rake-off for himself. And suddenly Jesus *has* something to declare: 'As he passed by, he saw Levi the son of Alphaeus sitting at the receipt of custom, and said unto him, Follow me' (14). This time it is Levi who pays: 'He arose and followed him' (14). And this time he gets the biggest rake-off of his life. He gets not only a Master, but a Friend. For Jesus now goes home to eat with him. And to share a meal, in the East, is a pledge of mutual support and loyalty, a sacred bond of friendship. It was not a private affair either, as if this were some exceptional favour conferred on Levi alone. For we are told there were a lot of other nasty types there too. It is not quite clear whether the meal was in Jesus' house or Levi's, and whether the others were Levi's camp-followers or were following Jesus independently. Probably it was Levi's house and Levi's friends. But at any rate they were all eating together: 'As Jesus sat at meat in his house, many publicans and sinners sat also together with Jesus and his disciples: for there were many, and they followed him' (15).

That, of course, was an unheard-of thing. Men like Levi were outcasts and regarded as beyond the pale. No doubt he would be one of Herod's customs officers, and therefore not quite so bad as the hated publicans who collected the Roman taxes. But he was still bad enough. He would be as dishonest as such officials always were. He would constantly defile himself by contact with Gentile traders. And worst of all, he would have to attend to anyone who wanted to cross the frontier on the Sabbath day. No good Jew would associate with a man like that. The only people who would befriend him were men as lax as himself, or worse. And now Jesus had gone over to join up with them all!

But when he did that, it was more than jumping the barrier between good and bad. There is something strangely ironic about a man named *Levi* living as this man did. For Levi in the Old Testament was the tribe that was set apart for the service of the sanctuary (Num. 1.49 ff; 18.2 ff; Deut. 10.8; 18.6 f). Levi was to have no possessions, because 'the Lord is his inheritance' (Deut. 10.9; 18.2), no business worries to distract attention from the service of God. Levi had a high calling (Num. 16.9): 'the law of truth was in his mouth, and iniquity was not found in his lips: he walked with God in peace and equity, and did turn many away from iniquity' (Mal. 2.6). But now here is a Levi who is all out for material possessions and cares little for his divine heritage, a Levi who is up to the neck in a business that automatically cuts him off from all part in the temple service. Here is a Levi who is classed with the lowest of the low, who scorns the 'law of truth' and far from turning others from evil only gathers a band of hangers-on as bad as himself. This Levi is the living contradiction of his name. He is the very embodiment of that grim picture in the book of Malachi —the picture of the mercenary sons of Levi who have so profaned their bond with God that he has cursed them and made them utterly 'contemptible and base before all the people' (Mal. 2.8 f). In our Levi it all takes flesh and blood. And his iniquitous campfollowers surely represent the others in the same prophecy—the rest of the Jews who followed the sons of Levi in the path of abomination and are therefore to be cut off along with them (Mal. 2.10-12).

When Jesus goes to *such* men, he crosses the most rigid barrier of all: the gulf that separates God from his reprobate people. And then another part of Malachi's prophecy is fulfilled. Priests and people alike, he had said, were so lost and cut off from God that there was no way back, and all their offerings and sacrifices only made matters worse. But Malachi had gone on to say: '*The Lord* shall suddenly come to his temple . . . and he shall purify the sons of Levi . . . that they may offer unto the Lord an offering in righteousness', and then the people who followed them will also be accepted again (Mal. 3.1-4). In the Gospel story we see that happening too: in Jesus the promised Lord also takes flesh and blood, Levi and his followers are restored, and the new service of God begins to take shape in the seamiest parts of a lost world.

So there is *no* limit to the breadth and depth of Christ's new order. It is for the church *and* the everyday world, the upper classes *and* the common people, the good *and* the bad. It is even for the perverse and ungodly and hopelessly lost.

But it is not allowed free course. There was no opposition from Levi and his like. They followed as they were told, without hesitation or excuse. There was no opposition from the disciples either. They were ready to go with their Master even when he led them into what must have been strange company for respectable men. But there were others—'scribes and Pharisees'—who objected strongly to what was going on. These men were theologians and pietists. They had studied the Bible until they knew most of it by heart. And they had learned from it such a passion for purity that they believed the one thing needful was to keep every detail of their lives free from defilement. There was plenty in the Bible that they could quote in support of that, and they expounded it all in a mass of detail, surrounding themselves with a multitude of rules and regulations which they called the 'hedge of the law'. They could then hurl threats of judgment at those outside. But if there was any *way* through the hedge, it was for one-way traffic only. Any outsider who would undertake to live as they did was welcome to come in. But it was forbidden to go out and join the wasters on the other side of the hedge. And now Jesus had the effrontery to do that. And at once these religious policemen were on to him. What did he think he was doing? This was clearly marked as a one-way street and he was going the forbidden way: 'When the scribes and Pharisees saw him eat with publicans and sinners, they said unto his disciples, How is it that he eateth and drinketh with publicans and sinners?' (16).

Jesus' answer could leave them little doubt as to what he thought he was doing: 'When Jesus heard it, he saith unto them, They that are whole have no need of the physician, but they that are sick: I came not to call the righteous, but sinners to a new life' (17). He did not pretend to be a stranger who did not know the rules. He did not say the law was wrong, or argue that there was really no difference between those who tried to keep it and those who did not. He merely said he was purposely throwing in his lot with the law-breakers, because they were sick and needed him. If

B

the guardians of the law were determined to stay inside the hedge and cultivate their own righteousness, then they could do it without him. He was going outside, and they must draw their own conclusions. And they did. You cannot fall foul of the law like that and get away with it. Just here, where we begin to see the full breadth and depth of the new order—just here we see also the strongest opposition to it, and the early shadows of the Cross. That was to be his penalty for taking the side of the law-breakers. There the last grim detail of Malachi's picture was to take a rather unexpected turn, and yet the only possible one: the terrible, searing fire of judgment which would purify the sons of Levi (Mal. 3.1 ff) was to fall on Jesus himself.

Now we have the full sweep of the Good News of the kingdom. Christ's new order is for every walk of life, for every class and condition of men, for all without exception who are willing simply to follow him. And he himself pays the price of our admittance. He has no delusions about the price. He does not pretend there are no serious barriers amongst us, no real difference between the sacred and the secular, no truth in our social and moral and religious distinctions. He sees all such barriers for what they are, and knows how sharply they divide us. But he breaks through them all, whatever it may cost him. He robs our differences of their old power to divide, and makes them contribute instead to the many-sided richness of one great new Family. Still he calls us, whatever our occupation or standing or worth or creed, to follow him. And still he gathers his true-hearted followers along with his perverse and sinful ones to eat with him at his table, and at ours.

But still there is opposition to it all. Some are all for clinging to their own position and achievements and maintaining the old barriers, or building new ones. These are the modern Pharisees, who delight to cultivate a private heaven behind some hedge and preach hell-fire and judgment at those outside. Not all modern Pharisees are in the church: many reject it, and their theme-song is, 'We do not need to go to church. For we are better than the hypocrites who do'. There you have the private hedge again, and the same harsh criticism of those on the other side. But we have no need to point, for we are all constantly tempted to take such self-satisfied attitudes. Only, it is time we realized that if we do it, then we do it without Christ. He will not be on *our* side of the fence, and we shall be doing one of the things that sent him to his Cross. That may be good enough for the synagogue and the sects and those who are always right. But it is not for the Christian church.

Nowadays we have also become familiar with another kind of opposition. For some insist on viewing the barriers from the other side. These are the people with the so-called inferiority complex. They say the demands of business and of home and all the many earthly claims of modern life leave them no room for religion and make it meaningless to them: they cannot follow Christ, because they are not spiritual enough. Or they are shy of their own insignificance, their lack of standing and influence and education: they cannot follow Christ, because they are not gifted enough. Or their conscience forbids them to pretend to a virtuous kind of life which they know they do not live: they cannot follow Christ because they are not good enough. Or they feel so God-forsaken that they doubt if God exists at all: they cannot follow Christ because they are not sure enough. Such hesitation looks so well with its air of humble honesty. We can all understand it, for we have all pleaded such excuses time and again. And yet it is utterly foolish. It is raising again all the barriers Christ has broken down and giving them a finality of which he has robbed them. It is slamming all the doors he has opened and shutting ourselves out of the kingdom he has brought. And for all its modern dress, it is an attitude as out-of-date as the other. For when Christ long ago offered his friendship to Levi and the rest, he made it crystal clear that his new order is *also* for the busy materialist, *also* for the unimportant, *also* for the bad, *also* even for the godless. In fact, he made it plain that it is *specially* for such people. And if Levi could go and follow him, then there is nothing on earth to prevent us all from doing the same.

Whatever else is true of us, there is one thing that is truer than any. And that is, that Christ is calling us again—each one of us— to follow him. Surely we shall not be so foolish as to resist him through pride or hesitate through false modesty. Surely we shall do the only sensible thing, and follow him as he says. That means, that from now on, in our work and in our homes, in our social life and our moral endeavours and our devotions, in all we suffer and all we do, *he* comes first and we come second. Then whatever experiences come our way—there will be plenty, both pleasant and otherwise—but whatever they may be, it will be life in the fullest sense, and a life that is always new. For this is the secret of all true life: it begins, continues and ends in following Christ. And he came to earth for no other reason but to call us to such life, and to make it possible for us.

Scene 5: *TRADITION AND CONSTRAINT*

And the disciples of John and of the Pharisees used to fast: and they come and say unto him, Why do the disciples of John and of the Pharisees fast, but thy disciples fast not? And Jesus said unto them, Can the children of the bridechamber fast, while the bridegroom is with them? as long as they have the bridegroom with them, they cannot fast. But the days will come, when the bridegroom shall be taken away from them, and then shall they fast in those days. No man also seweth a piece of new cloth on an old garment: else the new piece that filled it up taketh away from the old, and the rent is made worse. And no man putteth new wine into old bottles: else the new wine doth burst the bottles, and the wine is spilled, and the bottles will be marred: but new wine must be put into new bottles. (2.18-22)

Fasting is so much out of fashion nowadays that we are apt to wonder what all the fuss was about. But suppose some new teacher brought a band of young men to church, and they all came stamping in with their hats on and started chatting as if they were at the street corner, then surely most of us would be distinctly annoyed. There is nothing in the Bible which says a man must enter church reverently, hat in hand, and sit quietly composing himself until the service begins. It is simply the accepted thing to do. Just so, there is nothing in the Mosaic Law to demand fasting (except on the Day of Atonement). But in Jesus' time it was the done thing for a good Jew to fast two days a week. And like most traditions it was meant to serve a very laudable purpose. For one thing, it was an act of self-humiliation—putting yourself on bread and water like a criminal, to show that you recognized you were a criminal before God. It was also an act of self-discipline, intended to show that the spirit controlled the body's appetites and passions, even to the extent of mastering the craving for food. And it was surely a pretty good test of genuine piety. For it is easy enough to make a long prayer of confession, or to talk glibly about the superiority of the spirit. But if a man was serious enough about these things to go the length of deliberately refraining from food—and that twice a week—then it was a fairly safe guess that he really meant what he was saying. Not that all our Lord's contemporaries fasted. There were many who could not or would not. But everybody recognized that it was the thing for a pious man to do. So when Jesus' disciples apparently broke with the tradition, it is not surprising that people were indignant and asked him what they meant by it: 'Why do the disciples of John and of the Pharisees fast, but thy disciples fast not?' (18).

Jesus' answer, or the first part of it, was that for his disciples to fast would be completely out of place—as out of place as it would be for the guests at a wedding. In fact, it was really out of the question altogether. For 'the children of the bridechamber' (19) were the groomsmen, the inner circle of the bridegroom's friends. Nobody could expect the groomsmen at a wedding to fast, because on the contrary it was their special task to keep the feast going. And now, says Jesus, it was just as impossible for his disciples to fast at this stage. There is more in that picture than meets the eye. For Jesus is *the* Bridegroom in the Old Testament sense—the God who had long ago betrothed his people to himself and would one day come to claim Israel as his bride. In Jesus that promise was fulfilled. In him the Bridegroom was here, the wedding festival of Israel had already begun. And to suggest that his disciples should fast was only to show complete failure to understand what was happening.

He did not say fasting was wrong. In fact, he said there would come a time when the disciples would fast in no uncertain terms— when the Bridegroom would be taken away from them. And so indeed it was. It is hardly likely that they ate much between Good Friday and Easter Day. Even then it would not be a matter of self-humiliation or self-discipline: it would be an involuntary fast, simply because when your life starts crumbling about you the way theirs was doing then, you lose all taste for food. But meantime there was no place for anything like that. Now Christ was amongst them, and in his presence all is light and thrill and joy.

Why, then, do we so often give the impression that Christians are long-faced kill-joys, that our services are more like funerals than weddings, and our lives straitlaced and grim? There is a strange tradition amongst us that deals in terms of 'must' and 'must not': a Christian must not dance, must not play Sunday golf, must not laugh in church . . ., a Christian must read his Bible, must say his prayers, must regularly examine and discipline himself. . . . But how has that tradition been able to take root so firmly in the church? Why are we so ready to respect it, at least in its less bigoted forms? Is it because the Bridegroom has been taken away from us?—because we have become so tied up with ourselves and our own earnestness and respectability that we have lost sight of him? No doubt it is all very well meant. It springs from a desire to ensure reverence and purity and preserve the dignity of Christ. But it is utterly foreign to him. It cramps and restricts us and makes us like the guests at those horrible stiff weddings which nobody can enjoy, or like the type of best man who is so anxious always to do the right thing that he makes himself miserable and everyone else embarrassed. There is no place at all for that sort of thing in the presence of Christ. His gospel is *glad* tidings. Christian faith is a liberating, happy thing. If that is not obvious both in our church services and in our daily life, then plainly we have either lost him or completely failed to understand him.

Certainly there will be times when we stay away from entertainments, or neglect our comforts—just as the early disciples more than once found themselves too busy even to eat (3.20; 6.31). But there will be no compulsion in that: it will not be because we 'must' deny ourselves, but because our Master has kept us too wrapped up in other things to notice. There will also be times of deliberate sacrifice, and times of humiliation, and times when the going is so hard that we grit our teeth to battle on. But there will be no 'musts' there either. For these things are not duties imposed on us, but part of the privilege of serving Christ: because *he* asks it, the sacrifice is cheerfully made—because *he* trains us by it, the humiliation is hopefully borne—because *he* leads us in the battle, we go on with confidence despite our fears. The only days when there is any reason for gloom are the days when he is 'taken from us', or at least hides his presence. These will indeed be days of bitter constraint, when we *must* believe and cannot, must pray and know it for a mockery, must stumble on somehow where there is no way on. . . . Yet such days will be the great exceptions. For the rest, he will always be with us. And as long as we have him with us, then whatever happens there can be no place for grimness or constraint.

The second part of Jesus' answer was that for his disciples to fast would be not only out of place and impossible, but positively dangerous. If you patch an old coat with a piece of unshrunk cloth, then presently the patch will shrink and the tear will be made worse. If you put new wine into old skins which are already hard and stretched and have no more give in them, then the wine as it ferments and expands will burst the skins and in the end you only lose both. And that was really what the Pharisees were asking of the disciples in insisting that they should fast. They were asking them to retain the old well-worn practices, with a bit of new colour stitched on by Christ. They were asking them to confine the vital forces of Christ's new order within the rigid laws and traditions of the old. And that, says Jesus, would be a hopeless and foolish and dangerous task, which could only have disastrous consequences for both.

But is it not the very task we are all engaged on? For we, too, are such advocates of patchwork piety and lovers of old wineskins! We erect churches beside all the other buildings in our cities, put Bibles among the multifarious contents of our bookshelves, dress up our thinking with principles and phrases borrowed from Christ's teaching—and call the resulting patchwork a 'Christian civilization'. We form in the churches and round the Bibles congregations where so often what always has been must always be—and imagine that such hidebound groups are 'upholding the Christian tradition'. We expect Christ to approve of these things and call on him to help us in our efforts. But if only we would see the danger—the twofold danger—of it all! Surely the atomic age has already gone far enough to show that our 'Christian culture' is neither Christian nor cultured. For the only two atom bombs used till now were used by the 'Christian West'—not thoughtlessly, but after careful and conscientious deliberation— and the result is both to make Christianity suspect over wide areas of the earth and to leave us trembling for the very existence of our Western world. The patchwork thinking that uses biblical words and phrases with humanistic meanings has already gone far enough to make plain its danger both to the gospel and to humanity. For it not only takes the glory and power out of the gospel, but also creates so many intellectual difficulties that men are driven to choose between an irrational faith, which is inhuman, and an agnosticism that cuts them off from the only Source of true humanity. Surely, too, we have all seen enough stick-in-the-mud conservatism in church circles to know that any congregation that takes its stand on past tradition is heading for an eruption in which its own unity will be shattered and some promising new venture of faith lost.

There is no need to look far for evidence that the pursuit of patchwork piety and the love of old wineskins still leads to disaster, as our Lord said it would. The Jews he was speaking to ignored his warning, and the end was, that Judaism became a broken, useless thing and the gospel was lost—lost to them, at any rate, and taken to the Gentiles. If we go on as we are doing, the same thing will happen to us. Sometimes indeed one wonders if it has not already happened—if he has not already been compelled to take his gospel elsewhere and leave us to our own devices. But it is still not too late, if we will learn what he is trying to teach us here: that he has far better things for us than patches and past glories. Jesus is not a great Invisible Mender who fixes up the torn parts of life so that we may look a bit more respectable. Rather he comes to bring us a whole new life—a new culture in which our churches and Bibles play a central part instead of a decorative one, a new way of thinking in which our human reason is not sacrificed to 'faith' but begins to blossom under the hand of Christ. And this new life can never be bound by any traditions, however honourable: it constantly requires new methods, new forms of thought and practice, new ways of expressing its infinite richness and vitality.

There is still one more important thing to be learned, lest we should make the mistake of getting it all the wrong way round. It is only when the *Bridegroom* is with us that the grim religion of 'must' and 'must not' is ruled out, and only when we have *new wine* that new wineskins are required. There is no point in merely being determined to be bright and cheerful, and go in for the hearty, back-slapping, brother-how-I-love-you type of Christianity we sometimes hear about. It is no use simply throwing over old traditions for the fun of it, and introducing brighter services, new forms of worship, new and more interesting methods in our clubs and guilds. For if we set about it that way, then surely we are starting at the wrong end. A wedding party without a bridegroom would be a farce. And what use are new wineskins if all we have to put in them is coloured water, or wine that has gone flat? Jesus is not speaking here of what can happen when young men in high spirits turn their hand to religion, but of what happens when *he* appears on the scene. He is not talking about the new methods that may be called for by our bright ideas or by a gospel trimmed to suit them: he is talking of what is involved in the message *he* brings. It all comes from him, and can come from nowhere else. So what we need first and foremost is a new sense of the presence of Christ, a new grasp of the richness and vitality of his gospel. Once we have that, all the rest will follow naturally enough. As long as we have him with us, life will be an unconstrained and confident and happy thing, a thing of constant new discoveries, new ventures, new thrills.

SCENE 6: *THE SABBATH*

And it came to pass, that he went through the corn fields on the sabbath day; and his disciples began, as they went, to pluck the ears of corn. And the Pharisees said unto him, Behold, why do they on the sabbath day that which is not lawful? And he said unto them, Have ye never read what David did, when he had need, and was an hungred, he, and they that were with him? How he went into the house of God in the days of Abiathar the high priest, and did eat the shewbread, which is not lawful to eat but for the priests, and gave also to them which were with him? And he said unto them, The sabbath was made for man, and not man for the sabbath: Therefore the Son of man is Lord also of the sabbath. (2.23-28)

This question of the sabbath law still keeps cropping up every now and then. And it is one we usually find very difficult to answer. We have no great desire for a return to the grim Scottish Sabbath of earlier days. For even though we recognize that the pictures we have of it are often caricatures rather than truth, yet we feel that many of its rigidities must have been as much of a burden to God as they were to men. At the same time, though, we can hardly condone the total disregard of the fourth commandment in many circles today, and the way men actually welcome Sunday work because it means double pay, while vast numbers have no Sunday at all but only a 'week end'. Is there no alternative to these two attitudes? There is indeed. For here our Lord lifts us out of the dilemma and points us a new approach altogether.

It was something harmless enough that caused the argument: 'Jesus went through the corn fields on the sabbath day; and his disciples began, as they went, to pluck the ears of corn' (23). But for the Pharisees that amounted to reaping and was a breach of the sabbath law. I doubt if even the strictest sabbatarian today would argue that someone who picks a bunch of flowers during a Sunday walk is breaking the fourth commandment by working as a gardener or a botanist. We should call that following out the letter of the law to the point of absurdity. Yet Jesus does not dismiss the Pharisees' question as a ridiculous quibble. He gives them an answer. And in doing so he uses the type of argument every Rabbi was familiar with. First an example from 'The Prophets': 'David, when he had need and was an hungred, he, and they that were with him . . . went into the house of God . . . and did eat of the shewbread which is not lawful to eat but for the priests . . .' (26). Then an example from 'The Law': in the creation story, 'the sabbath was made for man, and not man for the sabbath' (27). And then a conclusion: 'Therefore the Son of man is Lord also of the sabbath' (28).

He does not mean, as many think, that there is good authority for giving human needs precedence over traditional laws, and for waiving the rigid observance of the sabbath where it would be a burden instead of a help. That would be saying something everybody knew already. For the Pharisees all agreed that exceptions could be made to the Law in case of special need, or for a special purpose. They had even worked out in detail what exceptions were permissible and when. The trouble was, plucking corn was not allowed for at all. And they would no doubt have said that if the disciples were hungry, there were other permissible ways of satisfying their hunger. For Jesus to have argued about that could only have meant a weary, fruitless discussion. For once you start playing off individual needs and wellbeing against general divine laws, then at once the question arises: how great must the need be in order to justify an exception to the rule? Then you are soon involved in legal cheese-paring and casuistry. And whatever Jesus intended, it could never have been that.

But he does not mean either, as others like to think, that every 'son of man', every child of the human race, is free to do as he likes with the sabbath. That would be to overlook something which anyone with a biblical mind must see at once. For according to the Bible, the man for whom the sabbath was made is no longer what he was. Adam (and 'Adam' is simply the Hebrew word for 'man') lost all his authority and was condemned to hard labour instead of the sabbath rest he had enjoyed. There is only one Son of Man who could now be called Lord of the sabbath. That is the one of whom the prophet Daniel speaks (Dan. 7.13 f): *the* Son of Man who is given all the dominion Adam once had—in other words, the Second Adam, the Messiah. And that is what Jesus is talking about here. He is saying: David could over-ride priestly tradition for the benefit of his followers, therefore the Son of David can do the same; Adam was free to use the sabbath which had been instituted for his sake, therefore the Second Adam's dominion includes lordship also of the sabbath. It should have been fairly easy for the Pharisees to grasp his meaning, for they were completely familiar with the biblical background and the terms used, and were well versed in that type of argument. Once they got that length, it was not a very big step to the inference: if Jesus now exercises this authority, then that surely indicates that Jesus himself *is* the Son of David and Son of Adam. No doubt it was still beyond them to see that. But *we* are supposed to know it. It was for us that Mark wrote the story down. And surely he tells it with a fine touch of dramatic irony: as the great dramatist so often does, he recounts a conversation whose real significance is lost on the actors, but well known to us in the audience. Here at any rate we are given a pointer to the true Christian attitude to the sabbath problem, and a sign of what was soon to be.

Christ, the Son of Man, is *Lord of the sabbath*. Therefore his disciples are not bound by the multifarious regulations with which sabbatarians ancient and modern try to encumber it. On the other hand, it is *Christ, the* Son of Man, who is Lord of the sabbath and not we ourselves. Therefore we are not left to the mercy of the anti-sabbatarians who maintain that each man has to find his own way. Here it is as if Jesus flung open a window and let in a gust of fresh air to relieve the usual stuffy atmosphere of discussions about sabbath observance. The one side stifles us with demands for blind obedience to some set of rules. The other side is just as oppressive with its insistence that each must be a law to himself and take the responsibility of solving the problem all alone. But here Christ points us to himself as the one who stands above all rules and bears all responsibility for us. And in his presence we can breathe freely again. He does not say: 'On this day you must rest from every kind of work.' Nor does he say: 'You must decide for yourselves what sabbath rest really means.' He says: 'Come unto me . . . and I will give you rest' (Matt. 11.28).

For wherever he is Lord, he rules *in order to give*. We have seen him as Lord of the body, giving back lost powers to the sick. We have seen how as Lord of the soul he gave pardon to sinners and restored the godless to friendship with God. Now we are told that he is 'Lord also of the sabbath', so it is only to be expected that here too he will restore a lost blessing. That, in fact, is what he does: as Lord of the sabbath he gives men back the sabbath as it was originally meant to be. In the story before us he does it already for his disciples in a small way, as a sort of foretaste of what he will later do in a much bigger way. That is our best key both to what is happening in this story, and to the whole meaning of the Christian sabbath already foreshadowed here.

If we are to be able to use the key, then first we must think for a moment of what the original creation sabbath was. It was a period of perfect *freedom*: there were no 'musts' in the Garden of Eden, but everything was 'may'. It was freedom for *fellowship*. For it was given not to one man but to a pair; and God, too, freed himself from his work of creation in order that nothing should hinder their communion with each other and with him. And it was freedom not for idleness, but for *service*. For man had the task of 'dressing the garden and keeping it' (Gen. 2.15). One thing, it is true, was forbidden: 'Of the tree of the knowledge of good and evil, thou shalt not eat of it: for in the day that thou eatest thereof thou shalt surely die' (Gen. 2.17). Yet that was not a limitation to man's freedom, but only a warning against losing it by trying to make his decisions without God. It was when man disregarded the warning that the catastrophe came. For in choosing self-dependence he made it necessary to be also self-supporting, and because he could not support himself he was bound to go under in the struggle. Now his freedom was lost, his fellowship broken, and his work became a burden and a curse. But God in his mercy did not leave man to his fate. He promised a Redeemer. And now in Jesus we see the Redeemer at work.

Adam's freedom on the first sabbath had been summed up in the words: 'I have given you every seed-bearing herb . . . and every fruit-tree . . . for meat. . . . Of every tree of the garden thou mayest freely eat' (Gen. 1.29; 2.16). Now Jesus on this later sabbath allows his disciples freely to pluck and eat the growing corn. Is it fanciful to find in that a first sign of the primeval freedom restored? Presently there will be another and better-known one. For he will go on to set the fruit of the vine alongside the corn, taking bread and wine together as the means of communicating the freedom he gives.

Here in the cornfield we also see something of the old fellowship being reasserted in a situation where everything makes for division. The Pharisees had come to Jesus with a complaint about his disciples—as previously (at Levi's house) they had gone to the disciples to complain of him. And everyone knows that talebearing is one of the simplest means of estranging friends. But Jesus uses the occasion to set himself all the closer to his disciples by firmly taking their part. Once more we have a pointer to what will happen later: when murder will be used to separate him from them once and for all, and instead he makes his death the beginning of a communion more intimate than ever.

The cornfield story also strikes again the note of freedom for service. Not only were these disciples Jesus' servants. But at this very moment, as the next verses show, they were on their way to a synagogue service where God was to be glorified and one of his creatures healed. That no doubt is one reason why Jesus will not suffer them to be detained by any carping criticism of the Pharisees—just as presently he will give them victory over every form of the sins which poison men's work and hinder their service.

Viewed in this light, the cornfield incident stands out clearly as a first sign of Christ's restoration of the sabbath. To be sure, it is only a beginning, a sign that awaits its fulfilment in the events of Good Friday and Easter. But here already we can catch the Good News of what the Christian sabbath means. For our sabbath, too, bears the same blessing and the same promise. It, too, is a new beginning that will one day be perfected.

It is Christ's gift to us, and it is meant to be a day of the greatest possible freedom. On this day we are to be free of all the many 'musts' and constraints that normally surround our lives—free to attend specially to our relations with God and our fellows—free to enjoy serving him and them. To lay down rules as to how it must be spent would be to deny all it stands for. We may spend it sometimes one way, sometimes another, entirely as the Spirit moves us. Of course, we shall want to be sure that it is *the* Spirit that moves us. For if it were after all only our own spirits urging us about some of our own ploys, then that would be to repeat Adam's mistake and risk losing all over again the great things this day brings. *The* Spirit—the Spirit of Christ who is Lord of the sabbath—

moves above all in Word and Sacrament. Therefore we shall want above all on this day to go where the Word is proclaimed and the Sacrament celebrated and there open our lives to his influence. It is not that churchgoing is suddenly laid on us as a new 'must' after all. But once we grasp the meaning of the Christian sabbath, then this is obviously the first and most natural way of using the freedom we are given. There is no better way of expressing too the fellowship and service which mark this day than by taking our place in the community which is assembled together for the service of worship. But whether we begin it that way or not, the whole day one way or another will be marked throughout by the same special freedom and fellowship and service.

And the day as a whole will also be a new beginning. So it was with the creation sabbath: it was on the seventh day that God rested from the work of creation, but his last work had been the creation of man and this was the first day of their life together. So it was again when Christ rested on the seventh day from the work of redemption which had ended with the re-creation of Good Friday, and then rose to bring the beginning not only of a new week but of a whole new age. That, incidentally, is why it is so appropriate both from the Old Testament and from the New Testament standpoint that the Christian sabbath is celebrated on the first day of our week. But the main point at the moment is that the things which mark this day do not simply end at sunset or midnight. A Sunday well spent will be followed by a week in which, even amid all the hampering and dividing and distracting influences of life, there is still something of the same freedom, still some new openness towards God and our fellows, still a new readiness to serve.

There are of course a great many questions in this. It is a question how much real freedom there is about our churchgoing, how much real togetherness in what happens here, how much worthwhile service. It is very questionable, too, how far these things characterize the rest of our Sunday and what real influence they have on the following week. At best we enjoy them only in part. Often we wonder if we have them at all. But here let us remember once more that it is *Christ* who is Lord of the sabbath, and our hope is in him, not in ourselves. The disciples in the cornfield were still far from the glorious life of the days after Easter. But already they were with Christ, and therefore it was only a matter of time until this early foretaste became the real thing. We too may be far enough from the full experience of all the Christian sabbath is meant to be. But we too are with Christ. If we have learned that he 'is Lord also of the sabbath' and that here, as everywhere, he uses his lordship to restore, then we shall now look to him in faith. And in that faith we know that in our Sunday worship and through the rest of the day he will grant us a real foretaste of that freedom and fellowship and service, we know he will enable us to take something of them into the week that follows, we know he will renew and deepen them for us every Sunday and every week, and we know it is only a question of time until at last they are perfected for us and the primeval sabbath in all its fullness restored.

SCENE 7: *REACTIONS*

And he entered again into the synagogue; and there was a man there which had a withered hand. And they watched him, whether he would heal him on the sabbath day; that they might accuse him. And he saith unto the man which had the withered hand, Stand forth. And he saith unto them, Is it lawful to do good on the sabbath days, or to do evil? to save life, or to kill? But they held their peace. And when he had looked round about on them with anger, being grieved for the hardness of their hearts, he saith unto the man, Stretch forth thine hand. And he stretched it out: and his hand was restored whole as the other. And the Pharisees went forth, and straightway took counsel with the Herodians against him, how they might destroy him.

But Jesus withdrew himself with his disciples to the sea: and a great multitude from Galilee followed him, and from Judaea, and from Jerusalem, and from Idumaea, and from beyond Jordan; and they about Tyre and Sidon, a great multitude, when they had heard what great things he did, came unto him. And he spake to his disciples, that a small ship should wait on him because of the multitude, lest they should throng him. For he had healed many; insomuch that they pressed upon him for to touch him, as many as had plagues. And unclean spirits, when they saw him, fell down before him, and cried, saying, Thou art the Son of God. And he straitly charged them that they should not make him known. (3.1-12)

'And they watched him . . . that they might accuse him' (2). How extraordinary that *that* could happen—that men could sit spying on Jesus in the hope of catching him out and finding a

way to get rid of him! And what makes it even more extraordinary is, that these were not particularly villainous or blackguardly
people: they were outstandingly good-living and respectable—in
fact, they were the church people of the day. The name 'Pharisees' probably means 'separated ones', 'people apart'. And what
set them apart was their zeal for churchgoing and Bible study,
their high principles and ideals and the real effort they usually
made to live up to them. But that was just the trouble: Jesus did
not fit in with their principles and ideals—and so they felt that
Jesus must be wrong. It was bad enough that he should do all the
things he had been doing: claim to forgive sins, ignore all the
recognized barriers, and disregard the tradition of fasting. But
now he had just defended his disciples for breaking the sabbath,
and for the Pharisees that was really going too far. For to them,
observing the sabbath was *the* great thing—so important that they
believed that if only all the people could be persuaded to keep one
single sabbath perfectly, then the kingdom of God would come.
They would have expected any new teacher to make common
cause with them at least on this point. And now it seemed that
Jesus had no intention of doing even that. That was what made
them so fighting mad and so determined that he must not be
allowed to go on. So when he gave them one more sign of his
refusal to join them in their view of the sabbath, they went off to
plot his destruction. But they only showed their own inability to
recognize the Messiah now that he was here. They only showed
that all their Bible reading had really got them nowhere, and their
whole imposing system of study and discipline was rotten at the
core. 'Whited sepulchres' Jesus once called them, outwardly beauti-
ful, but inwardly full of death and decay (Matt. 23.27). And now
he turned away, half in sorrow half in anger (5), and left them
altogether.

There is a solemn warning here for the respectable of every age.
Of course none of us would ever dream of trying to destroy Jesus.
But neither did these men at first! They began by 'reasoning in
their hearts' (2.6)—in other words, merely *thinking* something was
wrong when he made a claim which did not fit in with their own
ideas. Even when he went to eat at Levi's house, they only *asked
his disciples* what it all meant (2.16). It was not until the business
of fasting and sabbath observance that they came to Jesus himself
with serious objections, and not until he had openly 'broken the
sabbath' for the second time that they were stung into definite

action. So, it all starts with what we think of Christ in our hearts. It all begins with making silent reservations and objections when something about him does not fit in with our own preconceived ideas, assuming that our ways of thinking are certainly right and there must be something wrong with him when he does not accord with them. When we catch ourselves doing that, *then* is the time to take warning and beware. For then we are at the beginning of the slippery road that leads right down to the place where men quietly decide to get rid of him altogether. If we want a Church of the Whited Sepulchre, then that is one of the best ways of going about it. Merely start becoming indignant when Christ does not turn out to be all we expected, and then it will not be long until our churches, whatever they look like from the outside, are only empty tombs, where enquirers after Christ will find nothing at all —or only an 'angel' saying, 'He is not here. He is risen. He is away out in the world of men. This is only where they buried him.'

Out into the world of men. That is where he went when he left Pharisees: 'Jesus withdrew himself with his disciples to the sea' (7), to the place of trade and commerce, the focus of a fishing community's everyday life. There he got a better reception. There they flocked after him in masses from every quarter. It was only the common people—'a great multitude' of them from Galilee and all round about (7-8). But we might be happy to think that at least the masses received him better than their leaders did. And yet Jesus does not seem to have been entirely satisfied with their reaction either. He stayed with them. He taught and healed them. But he also kept his distance and prepared a way of escape if things should go wrong: 'He spake to his disciples that a small ship should wait on him . . . lest they should throng him' (9). He had good reason for that. And the reason is not far to seek. For it was obviously the old story of men following him for what they could get. They came because 'they had heard what great things he did' (8), because they wanted to see his miracles and be healed of their troubles. They sought him only as a great Healer and Wonder-worker. And although he would not for that reason turn them away, yet he had to keep his distance. As John's Gospel puts it in another place, he could not 'commit himself to them', for he knew only too well how unreliable they were (John 2.24).

There is surely a great deal of that 'multitude' in us all. For do we not many a time seek Christ only for his gifts? And precisely that is one of the things that make us such ineffective Christians. A faith based on curiosity or self-interest may look better than the opposition that comes of prejudice and preconceived ideas, but it is not so very different in the end. The multitude did not really understand Christ any better than the Pharisees. They were content to throng him as long as they got what they wanted. But the day came when they realized he was not going to give them that any more, and then in a fury of disappointment they joined the Pharisees in crying, 'Away with him, crucify him.' It took them longer than the Pharisees to reach that point, but they got there just the same. And so long as *we* persist in their kind of faith—so long as we follow Christ only, or mainly, for what we can get out of him—then we are in imminent danger of ending up there too. It is not that he will turn away from us. His mercy is far too great for that, and he will often give us far more than we could ever ask or expect. But as long as we persist in regarding him as merely the great Healer of human ills and weaknesses, we inevitably remain blind to what he really is. He cannot trust himself to us. He cannot admit us to that intimate and unhindered communion which is life indeed. And it is all too likely that sooner or later he will have to disappoint us so sorely that our acceptance will turn to bitter rejection.

But there was a third group there at the lakeside who were neither annoyed at Jesus nor in doubt as to what he was after. They are described as 'unclean spirits', or what we should call demented people. But like the madman we heard of before (1.24), they recognized who Jesus was. And they made no secret of it, but 'fell down before him and cried, saying, Thou art the Son of God' (11). We might think he would be glad to have a confession like that at last. But the strange thing is that he was not: 'He straitly charged them that they should not make him known' (12). I think we must read, 'that *they* should not make him known'. For these people—or rather, the demonic powers who controlled them—were *unclean* spirits. They recognized and acknowledged Jesus for what he was, but for all that they were determined to remain unclean. They were ready to fall down at his feet, ready to give him the highest of titles—but they had not the slightest intention of doing his will if they could possibly avoid it. In other words, they stand for the supreme type of pure lip-service. And that is a thing he simply does not want.

Is that not one of our own favourite reactions? Do we not, most of us, stand in the same condemnation? We worship and adore him on Sunday—but what about the rest of the week? We praise him with our lips—but what about our lives? It is not enough to 'believe' in him, not even to the extent of being ready to grovel at his feet: 'the devils also believe, and tremble, but . . . faith without works is dead' (James 2.19-20). We may speak of him in the very highest of terms, and often do. But if it is merely lip-service, it is not the slightest satisfaction to him. He sees it as a work of the devil. And his only response, if we have ears to hear it, is to tell us sharply that we should be better to hold our tongues.

But now, what if we recognize how strongly we are tied to our own prejudices and ideas, how deeply we are infected with blind self-interest, how prone we are to lip-service? Suppose we recognize how dreadfully these things frustrate and stultify our Christian lives? It is still so difficult, so impossible, for us to get away from them. So what then?

Well, then there is still another figure in our story, a figure of promise who stands there specially for us: 'There was a man there which had a withered hand' (1). And a withered hand is a far more significant thing that at first sight you might think. The hand in the Bible is the thing with which men act and work, help and serve. It is also the means of their intercourse with God—the thing with which they bring their gifts to the altar, the thing which they stretch out to God in prayer, the thing which is cleansed when they are forgiven. So a man with a withered hand was in a pretty bad way. He could think and study with the Pharisees. He could run with the crowd. He could talk as well as any. But these things did not get him anywhere. For he could not *do* anything. He was even hindered in his fellowship with God and hampered in his prayers. And there was no hope that he would ever be any better. For a withered hand is a withered hand and that is the end of it. But now he was in church and stood there before Christ. Now Christ said to him, 'Stretch forth thine hand' (5). He did as he was told—and was healed. So obviously there is something better than the highest of ideals, better than the deepest of aspirations, better than the finest of words. Better than all that is one little piece of practical obedience to Christ's command. For to that, be it ever so small and faltering a step, he responds with all his renewing and transforming power.

ACT II

Secrets of the Kingdom

SCENE 1: *THE NEW CREATION*

And he goeth up into a mountain, and calleth unto him whom he would: and they came unto him. And he ordained twelve, that they should be with him, and that he might send them forth to preach, And to have power to heal sicknesses, and to cast out devils: And Simon he surnamed Peter; And James the son of Zebedee, and John the brother of James; and he surnamed them Boanerges, which is, The sons of thunder: And Andrew, and Philip, and Bartholomew, and Matthew, and Thomas, and James the son of Alphaeus, and Thaddaeus, and Simon the Canaanite, And Judas Iscariot, which also betrayed him: and they went into an house. And the multitude cometh together again, so that they could not so much as eat bread. (3.13-20)

When Mark begins this Act by saying that 'Jesus goeth up into a mountain' (13), then that is more significant than it looks. For these words are not just a sort of stage direction setting the scene, or what many like to call an 'editorial connecting link'. On the contrary, they strike a note that is central and vital—one that belongs to the great 'up and down' rhythm that goes through the whole Gospel. Jesus here goes up to a mountain, and then down to an ordinary house. Later he will go up to a Cross, and down to a grave; up to new risen life, and down to share it with his disciples; up higher still to the very throne of God, and down again in the Spirit at Pentecost—with the promise of his coming down in person at the end of the ages to close the history of the world. Each time Jesus 'goes up', that brings a new stage in the story, a new turn to events. Here the 'going up into a mountain' opens the second Act of Mark's great drama. And with it there comes a subtle change of tone. For the scenes that now follow seem to be particularly full of double meanings: it is as if the 'veil of the flesh' wears thin and we are enabled to see not only the scenes themselves but also beyond them to the deep secrets of the kingdom. The things that now happen on the mountain top, at any rate, are more than ancient history. They are also pointers to what is happening still, high above the highest mountain top, at the seat of all authority, at the 'right hand of God'.

Look first of all here at Jesus himself. For the Act opens with him going 'up into a mountain', alone. Jesus, of course, has always been the centre of Mark's picture. In one scene after another he has shown us this Jesus moving sovereignly among men, Jesus calling, healing, teaching, striving by word and deed to open men's hearts to the new order of God's kingdom, Jesus amid the misunderstanding of his disciples, the opposition of the Pharisees, the short-lived approbation of the people, the lip-service of the unclean spirits. But now the question comes to be: what will he do in the face of this wholesale refractoriness? Now one brilliant spotlight falls on Jesus all by himself faced by this momentous decision. It is the same Jesus as moved through all the previous scenes—a man of flesh and blood with both feet planted firmly on this earth. We should probably want to add at once that he is clearly a very great man. But that is not what the spotlight suddenly picks out so plainly. A great man is one who by his very greatness points beyond and above himself to the eternal truths and realities of human existence. But Mark's spotlight shows us nothing of that. It shows only Jesus, and beyond and above him nothing at all—Jesus, with the Pharisees and the people and the disciples somewhere in the darkness below him, Jesus on whose decision now their whole future and their whole existence depends. That is surely our clearest glimpse so far of Jesus *the Son of God.* Here on the mountain he is high up, not just in terms of space, but in the sense that God is high above men. He is alone, not just without companions but without peers, as only God can be alone.

But—and this is the tremendous thing—he does not mean to *remain* in splendid isolation. The spotlight only shines for a second, but in that second the momentous decision is made: 'He calleth unto him whom he would; and they came unto him. And he ordained twelve, that they should be with him . . .' (13-14). On the face of it that could be the leader of a new movement asking for followers and appointing a small staff of lieutenants. Could be—but Mark clearly means us to see more in it than that. He chooses for 'call' the word commonly used of a court citing offenders or witnesses to appear before it—which indicates that this is not an invitation, but an authoritative, princely summons. He says, 'Jesus called whom *he* would', using an extra, barely translatable word to underline the 'he' and so emphasize that Jesus himself is the King in whose name the summons is issued. And he links the call and its answer so closely as to give the impression of an immediate, unhesitating response. These things all go to mark Jesus here not as the leader of a new movement, but as the God who speaks his sovereign word and it is done. The picture becomes even clearer with the ordination of the twelve. For the word used here for 'ordained' really means 'made' or 'created'—it is the same word as is used in Genesis of God's creating the world—and that suggests pretty plainly that the Jesus who 'ordains' them is God beginning the long-promised new creation. It does not then require much imagination to connect his choice of a group of twelve with the Old Testament choice of twelve tribes and to see his action as the beginning of a new Israel. And in that case the fact that he does it on a mountain may serve to identify him with the God who founded the old Israel on Mount Sinai. At any rate, it is plain enough one way and another that we are meant to see in these happenings on the mountain top a new act of the God who will not be alone.

God never did mean to be alone. That was why he created men in the first place for fellowship with himself. That was why he came in Jesus to win them back. And he does not now intend to be deterred by their recalcitrance. He has his own way of dealing with that. It is a quiet way, but one charged with divine power. It is not marked by the thunderings and lightnings in which that power was expressed on Sinai, but is more like the stillness in the beginning when the Spirit brooded over the deep and God said, 'Let there be', and there was. So it is here when Jesus contemplates the abyss of error and enmity and then speaks to call twelve men to him, and they come to him and he creates out of them the beginning of the new people of God. That is the first thing we have to see in these events on the mountain top. And that is what is also happening now above the highest mountain top. That is what he is doing now at the seat of all authority, at the 'right hand of God'. He is calling whom he will, enabling them to come to him, and creating them anew for himself.

The second thing we are shown here is: what sort of men

Christ chooses to share his life, and why. There was Simon Peter, big-hearted, quick-tongued, and thoroughly unreliable; James and John his fishing partners, who apparently had rather a good conceit of themselves; Andrew, who always seems to have hung in the background and may have had an inferiority complex; Philip, who can hardly yet have been out of his teens; Matthew the tax-gatherer, whom any good Jew would regard as a traitor to his country; Thomas the pessimist; one called 'the Canaanite', which was the name for a red-hot nationalist; a few who are mere names and nothing more; and Judas, whose only service was to start off the last act of the drama by his betrayal. We look in vain for anything outstanding about these men, or anything they had naturally in common. They are as ordinary and varied a company as you could find anywhere—men as like ourselves as they could well be.

But if that is so, why on earth did Jesus choose them? It is easy to say that he is the Lord who chooses whom he pleases and his reasons are no business of ours. But it is not necessary to smother our curiosity like that. For there is an answer here in the nicknames given to the three leaders: 'Simon he called Peter (the Rock), and James and John . . . he called Boanerges . . . Sons of Thunder' (16-17). There could be nothing less rock-like than the unstable, undependable Simon, and there is little indication that James and John had much of the thunderbolt or the firebrand about them. But Jesus was thinking, surely, of what they were to be. He needed a rock-like faith on which to build his church, and it was Simon who was to be given it. He needed men of fire and energy for his work, and he could make James and John such men. He saw that already, and that was enough for him, and in comparison with that, what they were at the moment did not matter at all.

So the new Israel began there on the mountain with twelve very ordinary men, chosen not for what they were, but for what under Christ they were to become. And once again that is what is happening now above the highest mountain top, at the 'right hand of God'. There Christ is calling the same sort of men still. Old or young, reliable or irresponsible, forward or shy, whatever our outlook on life or politics, whether we are important or mere nobodies—he calls us all without exception. And we need not stop to worry about our qualifications. For the test he applies is not what sort of raw material we are, not whether we are capable of doing great things for him, but simply whether he can make something of us. To be sure, he needs steadfast believers, and he needs regular firebrands. But the naturally credulous are not always the best believers, and the natural firebrands can easily burn for the wrong things. In any case, it is not because of anything we are that he calls us, but in order to make us into the right sort of believers and the right sort of firebrands and whatever else he needs. He knows he can do that, and we know he can do it, and therefore we can join him whatever we are.

The third thing Mark shows us here is the kind of life to which these men are now admitted. We are told Jesus 'ordained twelve *that they should be with him*' (14). And they are to be with him in every sense of the word. With him as pupils are with their Teacher, to be taught and trained by him; with him as followers with their Leader, to be guided and inspired by him; with him as protégés with their Patron, to be protected and upheld by him. They are to be with him as those who are on his side, ready to stand up for him through thick and thin. They are to be with him as servants with their Lord, to wait on him and be directed by him; and as a team with its Captain, to work together under him. They are to be with him as his constant companions, always there though others may come and go. Above all, they are to be with him in a unity so deep that he becomes their 'other self' or even their 'real self'—as Paul was later to put it, 'I live; yet not I, but Christ liveth in me' (Gal. 2.20).

Certainly, they are not merely to enjoy this wonderful, many-sided communion: 'He ordained twelve that they should be with him, *and that he might send them forth to preach, and to have power to heal sicknesses, and to cast out devils*' (14-15). For the new Israel, like the old, was not created for selfish privilege, but for missionary service. Christ is not content with twelve men, not even with a whole people. He wants *all* mankind. And it is as though he works on the principle of 'set a thief to catch a thief'. When he has a message to win men, he sends men to deliver it. When he wants healing and help brought to them, he sends men to bring it. That is what these twelve men are there for: they are not meant just to regale themselves with Jesus on the mountain top, but are to be sent out to take his blessings also to others. And yet—and this is very important—their communion with him does not end where their mission begins. Even when he sends them forth, they will still be with him. Otherwise they could achieve nothing. When Peter one day ventures his own ideas about the kingdom, Jesus will call him a devil (8.33). When the twelve set out on the lake by themselves, they will make no headway against the storm (6.48), or when nine of them try on their own to cure an epileptic child, it will be a miserable failure (9.18). And when they are separated from their Lord on Good Friday there will not be a single thing they can say or do. Only when they are with him will they be able to fulfil their mission. But as long as they are with him, whether in the flesh or in the Spirit, they will preach and they will heal and the results will be astounding. So the new life of these men does not fall into two separate parts—a communion with Christ and a mission to the world. It is from first to last communion with him. But it is a communion which enables them to glorify him as well as to enjoy him for ever.

That is the third thing about this scene on the mountain. And once more it points beyond itself, beyond the highest mountain top, to the great secret of the church's life. For in such communion with the exalted Christ is the essence of all Christian life, and the glory of it. We, too, are with him as our Teacher and Lord, our Patron and our Cause—and are thereby freed from the dire necessity of deciding between the many conflicting offers of enlightenment and inspiration, the many different promises of security, the many good causes competing for our service. We, too, are with him as the Lord who has quietly taken over control of our lives and so released us from the burden of having to be our own masters; and as our Captain who can resolve our many differences and mould us into a true community. We are with him as the constant Companion whose presence makes life a thing of unlimited possibilities and ever-new horizons. We are with him in that intimate union in which he becomes our 'true self', so that even humiliations have the dignity of his sufferings and every dark place is lit with the certainty of his triumph. And then there is also his great commission to us, which adds to all these blessings the thrill of having a message to proclaim and a task to do. But that, too, is simply another aspect of life *with* him. We are not suddenly sent off by ourselves to speak to men and to help them, or we should soon become bogged down in mediocrities and frustrations. It is in communion with him that we carry out our commission, as it is in communion with him that we receive it. And with him we shall always find something to say that is worth saying, something to do that brings real help.

No doubt most of us would hesitate to picture our own lives like that, for we so often live in shadows that obscure the truth from us. No doubt, too, the whole truth is strictly not to be seen at all but can only be grasped in faith, for (meantime at any rate) it is 'hid with Christ in God' (Col. 3.3). But it is surely well for us if this scene on the mountain can raise us to new faith and give us a new vision of our life as it is meant to be—as, in Christ, it really is.

Only—and this is the last thing Mark would urge on us here— the vision is not meant to be contemplated with idle longing, but to be lived by and in some sort realized. Jesus did not keep the twelve up there on the mountain side enjoying their new privileges and planning a great missionary campaign. He came right down with them 'into a house' (19) and got going with the work at once.

That was always his way, and always will be. When he had called Simon at the lakeside long before, he then went home with Simon (1.16, 29). As soon as he had called Levi, he went to Levi's house (2.14 f). Here the call of the twelve on the mountain top ends with their all going home together. And it will be no different for us. He has bidden us rise in mind and heart and spirit far beyond the highest mountain to his own throne 'at the right hand of God'. He has called us there to share his life and be his envoys. Now he goes down again with us in the Spirit, back to our own houses to work it all out in the life of everyday.

We are told that working it out kept the disciples so busy 'that they could not so much as eat bread' (20). And it may very well be so also for us. For he and his work take precedence over everything else. We may often find ourselves missing things that seemed of great importance to us—sometimes perhaps even a meal or two. But that does not really matter. What matters is Jesus Christ, first, last and all the time. What matters is, that we should have the faith to stick by him and the fire to stick up for him. He was able to create that faith and that fire in the first disciples. He is just as able still.

SCENE 2: *MINDS AND FEELINGS*

And when his friends heard of it, they went out to lay hold on him: for they said, He is beside himself.

And the scribes which came down from Jerusalem said, He hath Beelzebub, and by the prince of the devils casteth he out devils. And he called them unto him, and said unto them in parables, How can Satan cast out Satan? And if a kingdom be divided against itself, that kingdom cannot stand. And if a house be divided against itself, that house cannot stand. And if Satan rise up against himself, and be divided, he cannot stand, but hath an end. No man can enter into a strong man's house, and spoil his goods, except he will first bind the strong man; and then he will spoil his house. Verily I say unto you, All sins shall be forgiven unto the sons of men, and blasphemies wherewith soever they shall blaspheme: But he that shall blaspheme against the Holy Ghost hath never forgiveness, but is in danger of eternal damnation: because they said, He hath an unclean spirit.

There came then his brethren and his mother, and, standing without, sent unto him, calling him. And the multitude sat about him, and they said unto him, Behold, thy mother and thy brethren without seek for thee. And he answered them, saying, Who is my mother, or my brethren? And he looked round about on them which sat about him, and said, Behold my mother and my brethren! For whosoever shall do the will of God, the same is my brother, and my sister, and mother. (3.21-35)

'When Jesus' friends heard of it, they went out to lay hold on him; for they said, He is beside himself' (21). These people were his nearest relations ('friends' is hardly the right translation) and their attitude is understandable enough considering what they were hearing about him. This son and brother of theirs drawing such enormous crowds after him and saying and doing such extraordinary things—that was upsetting enough for a respectable village family. But the doubtful and dangerous types he was associating with, and the way he persisted in crossing swords with the Rabbis, and now making grandiose plans with an organized band of followers, and even neglecting his meals! Surely that was going too far. His reforming zeal must have gone to his head. This was some strange kind of religious ecstasy. It was sheer madness which could only end in serious trouble. There were enough dark rumours going about already. He might soon get himself excommunicated, perhaps even killed. And that would mean disaster for him and disgrace for them. How were they to know that he *was* going to get himself excommunicated and killed? How were they to know that it was not madness but all part of God's amazing plan, and that if they tried to prevent it they would really be joining the opposition? They never stopped for a moment even to think of anything like that, but only felt what anyone with natural family feelings would have felt—that this was no way for a member of their family to behave. They must give him a chance to cool off, and get him to tone down his claims. So off they set to Capernaum to fetch him home.

Meanwhile in Capernaum itself the local Rabbis had got a group of theological professors down from Jerusalem to see what *they* could make of it all. And they hit on another explanation. Jesus was not just going too far; he was going utterly wrong. It was not madness but black magic. 'The scribes which came down from Jerusalem said, He hath Beelzebul, and by the prince of the devils casteth he out devils' (22). No doubt it was a shockingly malicious argument. But it was clever. It was so logical and looked so well. Everyone knows all is not gold that glitters. They could point to the way Pharaoh's sorcerers had performed the same miracles as Moses (Ex. 7.11; 8.7) and to the well-known warning that a prophet's signs do not automatically guarantee his authenticity (Deut. 13.1-3). As the Christians put it later, the Antichrist would work as great wonders as the Christ (II Thess. 2.9; Rev. 13.13). Or as we often see in our own day, the latest wonder drug may not always be such a blessing after all, once all its side-effects are discovered. And it was not only a clever argument. It also had all their authority behind it as the recognized leading thinkers of the day.

So it was not only the common people and the country Rabbis who got Jesus wrong. The circle of opposition narrows to include the warmest hearts of his own family, and widens to include the cleverest heads of the intellectuals from the capital—the one anxious for his wellbeing and their own good name, the others using their cleverness to explain him away and find reasons for rejecting what they did not want to see. With that the circle of opposition is about as complete as it could be. Mark could have given no clearer indication that *wherever* you put this Jesus, he simply does not fit in. Everywhere he is a stranger, a renegade, an offence.

We, of course, do not see him like that—not we, with our long church tradition and our Christian civilization and our Christian world. We find ourselves quite at home with him—stimulated perhaps, sometimes even challenged, but certainly not upset or offended or annoyed. Yet that is precisely what is wrong with us.

And it would be well for us if this story could shake us into realizing that still, even in our Christian world, he is as much a misfit as ever he was. The fact is, we only get on so well with him because we have had such long practice in doing what these people were trying to do—toning down everything that offends our susceptibilities or getting our clever minds on to explaining away whatever it does not suit us to have true. But he will not be dealt with either way. Rather he takes the initiative into his own hands. And whether our intentions are good or bad, he deals devastatingly both with our feelings and with our minds when they try to lay down the law to him.

The clever ones got their answer first: dog doesn't eat dog—or as he put it, 'How can Satan cast out Satan?' (23). Incidentally, he seems to be indulging in a good-humoured word-play on their own expressions, 'king of the devils' and 'Beelzebul' which apparently means 'Lord of the house'. 'If a *kingdom* be divided against itself, that kingdom cannot stand. And if a *house* be divided against itself, that house cannot stand. And if Satan rise up against himself, and be divided, he cannot stand, but hath an end' (24-6). And if you see a 'strong man's house' being plundered, then the inference is that someone stronger than the Lord of the house has taken control (27). That, too, was logical enough. And yet it was not exactly a watertight argument. It was surely just as logical to say that Satan was not rising up against himself, but only reorganizing his forces for the sake of a better come-back, driving out some of his inferior minions to make room for 'seven other devils worse than the first'. A dictator sometimes carries out a purge in his own camp, and householders have been known to work hand-in-glove with a thief in order to cash in on a big insurance claim. That, in fact, was precisely the sort of thing that the scribes alleged was going on between Jesus and the devil in all these cures and exorcisms.

There is really no arguing with that sort of thing. And Jesus did not try. He gave them not argument, but what Mark calls 'parables' (23). And parables are simple riddles which show us the truth only if we like to look the way they point. If these professors liked to look, they could see well enough that this was too big a thing to be even a major political purge in Satan's realm: it was a wholesale rout of all the powers of evil in every form. If they liked to look, they could see that the strong man had obviously been

bound against his will. And if they liked (for they knew their
scripture as well as anybody) they could remember Isaiah's promise that when that happened, it would be the work of God himself (Isa. 49.24 f). So the truth was that Jesus had declared total
war on the whole kingdom of evil, that he had already mastered it
and was delivering men from its power, and that what he was
doing was none other than the work of the Spirit of God. It
would require a fundamental change in their whole attitude to him
if they were to see that and accept it. But if they refused, if they
preferred to stick to their guns, then they were really calling the
Holy Spirit the devil. And that, he concludes, is the one unforgivable sin (29). For that is the most frightful thing about the
attitude they were adopting: that it puts an inevitable stop to the
whole unfolding of the gospel promise. The motorist who insists
that green is red will never get past the first traffic light. And as
long as a man persists in an attitude which implies that the Spirit
of Christ is the devil, he cuts himself off from all possibility of
progress or pardon.

We are not told whether the professors learned their lesson. But
the really important question is, whether we learn ours. We may
readily grant that the forces of evil are not divided. For it surely
requires no great ingenuity today to see how they play into each
other's hands and all work together to make havoc of our world—
the demons of falsehood, suspicion and fear, the demons of greed
and oppression, the demons of thoughtlessness, of envy and dis-
sension, and the great demon of self, to mention only a few. We
see them all clearly enough at work, and we take them all very
seriously. But—what about the Christ who has declared war on
the lot, who has bound them and is releasing men from their
power? We do not see so much of him. We do not see him because
we do not *want* to—not where he is dealing with our own particular favourite demon, and if we will not see him there, then we
shall not see him anywhere else either. It is not pure malice that
blinds us to him, as it seems to have been with the scribes. It may
be weakness or misunderstanding or ignorance. It may be care-
lessness or indifference. It may be that we are self-satisfied and
easy-going and do not want to be disturbed. But these things are
sins. They bring us into mortal danger, because they obscure the
Christ from us and obstruct the unfolding of his promises. They
are not the one unforgivable sin that puts a full stop to the whole
process of our salvation. They belong among all the other sins

which he says can be forgiven: 'Verily I say unto you, All sins shall be forgiven unto the sons of men, and blasphemies wherewith soever they shall blaspheme' (28). But he did not mean they are insignificant or to be taken lightly. They are not. And here he calls us to abandon them, to change our attitude as completely as the scribes were called to change theirs. He presents himself to us as the Lord who has bound all the forces of evil and means to free us from their power. He bids us stop finding reasons for taking the demons in general and our own favourite demons in particular more seriously than himself, and concentrate all our attention and respect on him.

But we must take him just as he is. There is no use trying to tone down any of his claims, not even when they hurt. And often enough they do hurt, especially in the realm of natural likes and dislikes. That is made startlingly clear in his answer to the members of his family, who by this time had arrived to exercise their influence on him both for his good and for theirs. 'Who,' he asks, 'is my mother, or my brethren?' (33). *Not* at any rate those who let their natural affection interfere with the doing of the Father's will in the Father's way. When that happens, then even if it be his own kith and kin he repudiates all family relationship with an abruptness and decisiveness that leaves no room for doubt. We are all endowed with different ties of blood and kinship and upbringing, and a vast array of sympathies and antipathies which naturally arise from them. It is well that it should be so, for God does not want a world of mass-produced creatures all mechanically toeing the same party-line. But just as with every thought, so too every feeling must be made subject to Christ. Our natural likes and dislikes must be bent to suit his purposes, not he to them. That is the one thing needful and the one tie that binds together the true family of Christ: 'Looking around on them which sat about him, he said, Behold my mother and my brethren! For whosoever shall do the will of God, the same is my brother, and my sister, and mother' (34-5).

'Whosoever shall do the will of God'—that can hardly mean just keeping particular commandments or living by a set of rules. After all, the disciples at the moment were not really 'doing' anything at all in the usual sense of the word, but were only sitting around watching Jesus and listening to him—just as Mary was only sitting at his feet when he said she was doing the one thing needful (Luke 10.39 ff). If we ask what, then, is this will of God that they were doing and we are also to do, then probably the best answer would be the one Jesus himself gave on another occasion: 'This is the will of him that sent me, that every one that seeth the Son, and believeth on him, should have everlasting life' (John 6.40). To see the Son, to believe on him, and to have everlasting life—that in a single sentence is the great summons of this whole passage. We are to look to Jesus and see him for what he is: the Son of God who binds the 'strong man' and frees his household, who declares war on him also where he tries to work subtly through the natural sympathies and antipathies of men. We are to believe in him, to take him utterly seriously in humble trust, and flout the forces of evil instead of showing such respect towards them. And with that vision and that faith we are to begin living with him—in the world he has conquered and the great family he has founded—the life which is life eternal.

SCENE 3: *HEARING THE WORD*

And he began again to teach by the sea side: and there was gathered unto him a great multitude, so that he entered into a ship, and sat in the sea; and the whole multitude was by the sea on the land. And he taught them many things by parables, and said unto them in his doctrine, Hearken; Behold, there went out a sower to sow: And it came to pass, as he sowed, some fell by the way side, and the fowls of the air came and devoured it up. And some fell on stony ground, where it had not much earth; and immediately it sprang up, because it had no depth of earth: But when the sun was up, it was scorched; and because it had no root, it withered away. And some fell among thorns, and the thorns grew up, and choked it, and it yielded no fruit. And other fell on good ground, and did yield fruit that sprang up and increased; and brought forth, some thirty, and some sixty, and some an hundred. And he said unto them, He that hath ears to hear, let him hear.

And when he was alone, they that were about him with the twelve asked of him the parable. And he said unto them, Unto you it is given to know the mystery of the kingdom of God: but unto them that are without, all these things are done in parables: That seeing they may see, and not perceive; and hearing they may hear, and not understand; lest at any time they should be converted, and their sins should be forgiven them. And he said unto them, Know ye not this parable? and how then will ye know all parables?

The sower soweth the word. And these are they by the way side, where the word is sown; but when they have heard, Satan cometh immediately, and taketh away the word that was sown in their hearts. And these are they likewise which are sown on stony ground; who, when they have heard the word, immediately receive it with gladness; And have no root in themselves, and so endure but for a time: afterward, when affliction or persecution ariseth for the word's sake, immediately they are offended. And these are they which are sown among thorns; such as hear the word, And the cares of this world, and the deceitfulness of riches, and the lusts of other things entering in, choke the word, and it becometh unfruitful. And these are they which are sown on good ground; such as hear the word, and receive it, and bring forth fruit, some thirtyfold, some sixty, and some an hundred.

And he said unto them, Is a candle brought to be put under a bushel, or under a bed? and not to be set on a candlestick? For there is nothing hid, which shall not be manifested; neither was any thing kept secret, but that it should come abroad. If any man have ears to hear, let him hear. And he said unto them, Take heed what ye hear: with what measure ye mete, it shall be measured to you: and unto you that hear shall more be given. For he that hath, to him shall be given: and he that hath not, from him shall be taken even that which he hath. (4.1-25)

When Jesus tried to teach men, he did not use long, involved arguments which you can only understand after five years at university (and perhaps not even then). 'He taught them in *parables*' (2), which clothed what he had to say in the simplest of terms. And he based his parables on the things most familiar to his hearers. When he was dealing with Bible experts, he pointed them to a story about David (2.25), or a passage about the sabbath (2.27), or a prophetic promise (3.27). When he taught the common people, he spoke of seeds and candles, popular proverbs, and ordinary everyday things. That is one of the great things about his teaching: that it brought the truth right home to the hearer's door.

But he also makes it very plain that he will not force it *through* the door. He is ready to give us the truth in digestible form, but he will not spoon-feed us. He speaks in ways anyone can understand, but that makes it all the more important that we should *listen* to what he says: 'He taught them many things by parables, and said unto them in his teaching: *Hearken*' (2-3). And he repeats it again and again: 'Hearken, listen, take heed what you hear', or (it may be) 'take heed how you hear'. A sower goes out sowing, but after

C

that all kinds of things can happen. The mere fact that he goes sowing is no guarantee that the seed will grow. And so it is also with Jesus: the mere fact that he comes preaching and teaching is no guarantee that anything will come of it. What he says must be heard—really heard and grasped and appropriated, if we are to have any lasting benefit from it. So if you have ears in your head, listen! Listen with all the ears you have!

We might wonder why he is so very emphatic and insistent about it. But the point is, as he explained to his disciples, that there is a 'mystery' (11), a secret in all this—the mystery of the God whose ways are not in the least our ways and his thoughts far other than our thoughts, the secret of his new order that is already bursting in all round us though we may not see the slightest sign of it. These are the deep things Jesus is teaching about, and the pictures he uses to illustrate them have something mysterious about them too. They are seldom mere telling illustrations. They are more like the puzzle pictures we used to get as children—quite ordinary pictures to all appearance, but when we looked carefully and turned them this way and that, we found they contained all kinds of hidden faces or animals or fruits or whatever it might be. So much of Jesus' teaching is like that—puzzle pictures, stories with a hidden meaning. It may be only one thing that is hidden in a particular story, or it may be several. But everything depends on whether we discover it or not. We can if we want to, for he makes it easy enough. But it may be that for one reason or another we do *not* want to.

If that should happen, then the parables that could have helped us will serve a different purpose. Instead of initiating us further into the truth, they will remain riddles to us and so brand us as 'outsiders'. They will make it plain that, like the people of Isaiah's day, we choose to see without perceiving and hear without understanding and so remain unrepentant and unforgiven (12, cf. Isa. 6.9-10). And that is surely worse than to have missed the truth altogether. The fact is, Jesus' teaching is always double-edged. It will help us or harden us, according to the attitude we adopt. It brings the vast hidden truths of God's sovereignty and ways down to a level where we can grasp them or not as we please—and are judged accordingly. We can hardly be blamed for sleeping through an abstruse sermon, or for failing to understand Plato or Kant or Heidegger. But we can and shall be blamed if we do not understand Jesus' teaching when it puts the truth so well within our grasp. That is why it is so crucially important that we should concentrate all our attention on hearing what he says.

But have we not heard it all often enough? May be—but it depends how and what we hear. That, he says, is completely fundamental. If we do not grasp this point, we shall never grasp any of the others (13). If we do not get this business of hearing right and learn to hear properly, then we shall never get anywhere at all. The thing is, there are so many different ways of hearing.

We can hear only with our ears—the way we hear the words of so-called 'polite conversation', or listen, say, to a radio variety programme. And then it does not really mean a thing, but all simply goes in one ear and out the other. 'Some fell on the footpath, and the fowls of the air came and devoured it up' (4).

Or we can hear Jesus' words (shall I say?) only with our mind—as we listen to the words of a great teacher or respected leader who summons men to higher things. And then it may all inspire us, perhaps even thrill us—until it is contradicted by some apparently better theory, or by the hard facts of life. 'Some fell on rocky ground, where it had not much earth; and immediately it sprang up, because it had no depth of earth. But when the sun was up it was scorched; and because it had no root, it withered away' (5-6).

Or we can hear the way we hear the latest sensation that stirs us, or a touching 'good cause' appeal that goes right to our heart. And there is certainly plenty that is sensational and plenty that is appealing about Jesus' teaching—or would be, if we had not got so used to it all. But that does not last either: the great sensation soon passes, and so do the various good resolutions, because life is too short and there are so many other things competing for our attention. 'Some fell among thistles, and the thistles grew up, and choked it, and it yielded no fruit' (7).

But now, suppose I were listening to a variety programme, and then to an inspiring talk by some eminent leader, and then to a sensational news bulletin or some moving appeal, and then all of a sudden the announcer said, 'Here is an S.O.S. message for . . .', and I heard my own name and that one of my nearest relatives was desperately ill. Then surely it would be very different. This means me! And my ears *and* mind *and* heart and everything else would fairly get going at once. That is the only sort of hearing that really gets into us and makes a lasting impression. And that is how Christ wants his teaching to be heard—not just with ears, or mind, or heart, but so that it gets right down into our being and becomes the driving force of all our thinking and feeling and our whole life. 'Some fell on good ground, and did yield fruit that sprang up and increased; and brought forth, some thirty, and some sixty, and some an hundred' (8).

There can be no doubt at all that Jesus means us to hear him that way. The sower does not scatter his seed expecting nothing to happen; he intends it to grow. Or to take another picture (21), a man may buy a candle and store it somewhere out of the way— under his meal-measure or under the bed. But that is not what he buys it for: he means it to be put on a candlestick in the evening and give him light. So, too, when Christ clothed his teaching in simple riddles, he did not intend them to remain riddles. Still less did he mean them just to be written down by someone in a Bible and be stowed away in people's bookshelves and forgotten about. He meant them to be examined with all the attention we can muster, in order that they might be solved, and so cast light on the all-important mystery of God's sovereignty and ways. So once again, he says, be careful in this critical matter of hearing: 'Take heed how you hear' (24). For the better you hear, the more light you will get: 'with whatever measure you mete, it shall be measured to you'; and if you take the trouble to listen properly, you will not only be shown the answer to the little puzzles, but you will also be enabled to understand the great secret of God's new order here in this world of ours and to take your part in it.

It is a simple common-place of everyday life that the rich not only get interest on their investments, but get power and influence and respect as well, whereas the poor have to pay out their money as soon as it comes in, and have no influence and probably lose even their self-respect: 'He that hath, to him shall be given: and he that hath not, from him shall be taken even that which he hath' (25). Jesus does not say that is a good thing or a bad thing. He simply points to it as a well-known fact and says it is much the same with his message. The better we take it in, the deeper the understanding we shall be given and the more wonderful our life will become. But if we are poor listeners, if we listen only inattentively, or superficially, or half-heartedly, then we shall be worse off than if we had never heard it at all. For we shall be missing everything that makes life really worth while. And it will be entirely our own fault.

That is surely the immediate message of these parables. But perhaps there is also a deeper meaning in them—for us, at any rate, if not for the first hearers. Perhaps Jesus is doing more here than merely urging us to listen to what he says as a matter of life and death. Almost any prophet or preacher of God's word would urge that on us, and would be right to do so. For wherever that word is proclaimed, we are put in the same critical situation. Even the Old Testament Preacher knew that when he issued his solemn warning: 'Watch your step when you go to the house of God, and be more ready to *hear* than to make foolish offerings, rash prayers, or hasty vows' (Eccles 5.1 f). But Jesus does not only preach God's word: he *is* the word in human flesh. He does not only tell us about God and his new order. He *is* God, though he may not look like it. He *brings* the new kingdom on earth, though it may not be obvious at once what he is doing. And these parables are not only about his message, but about himself.

This is not just a great Teacher going about like the sower and scattering his words everywhere to be heard by all and sundry. Here is Jesus the Son of God, giving *himself* everywhere and to the uttermost for men. But if the mere fact of sowing is no guarantee that the seed will grow, neither is Jesus' presence alone any guarantee that men will accept him for what he is. He is here, God with us—but who will penetrate his secret? He is here among us—and by our attitude to him we are judged. A God who lives away 'up in heaven' is quite a convenient God. It may be interesting to hear about him, as it is interesting to hear, say, of the doings of the royal family, yet it does not really concern us very much. We cannot go up to heaven to share his life, any more than we can walk in and out of the royal palace at will. But if the Queen were suddenly to knock at your door and say she had come incognito to pay you a personal visit, then it would make all the difference whether you recognized her and what you did about it. And when God comes down in Jesus to our own level to meet us as man-to-man, then that is no longer just convenient or interesting, but we are faced with a vital and urgent decision. Then we have to make up our minds about him, for good or for ill. Then everything depends on whether we get him right. And one way or another it is so easy to get him wrong.

We may regard him simply as someone who said and did quite extraordinary things two thousand years ago—one of the great figures of history, perhaps the greatest of them all. That, in fact, is the way most of us do think of him at first. For whenever we hear the name Jesus, do we not immediately picture a man in strange oriental clothes who lived in Palestine so long ago that it might just as well have been any time, because we cannot really sense how long ago it was? It is certainly important that he lived when and where he did. But unless we can find a great deal more to it than that, we shall be heading for immediate disaster. We may do our best to picture him as he really was. We may try to trace his influence on the world history in which we have our own little part. But not even the greatest figure of the past can have any living contact with us today. A Jesus who is only a distant shadow is little better than none at all. What real meaning can he have for us, if as soon as he is presented to us he is suddenly whisked away back down the ages until he is separated from us by a wide gulf of space and time? If that should happen, then the devil himself is at work, using the simplest and easiest method of making Christ meaningless. 'These are they by the way side, where the word is sown; but when they have heard, Satan cometh immediately, and taketh away the Christ who was sown in their hearts' (15).

But now, here is another attitude we may take. We may find in Jesus some sort of God who brings the promise of an ideal kingdom of universal peace and blessedness. Then we may well be fired and thrilled by it all and feel we have something to live for. For that is a Jesus who is likely to appeal to most of us. We all have our ideals and our dreams of happiness. We may be glad of a God who will make them come true, and we may well be ready also to do our part. Yet if that is all we have, then the fire and the thrill cannot last for very long. A mere God is too much of a heavenly being and not close enough to men. Ideal kingdoms are like castles in the air that have no proper roots in this earth. When it comes to putting it all into practice, we find so many difficulties that it just doesn't work. And then we feel frustrated and disillusioned and start looking for other ideals that are easier to attain. 'These are they likewise which are sown on rocky ground; who, when they have heard the word, immediately receive it with gladness; but the thing has no root in themselves, and so they endure but for a time: afterward, when affliction or persecution ariseth for the word's sake, immediately they are offended' (16-17). A superhuman Christ is not much better than a shadow Jesus after all. He must be firmly planted and rooted in our human world if our human Christianity is to be lasting and stand up to the stress and strain of life.

And yet we must not try to restrict him to this world of ours. For that is still another way of getting him wrong. So many see in him only the great Reformer of moral and social evils, the great Example of human life at its finest. And if we take him that way, then we may set out to follow his example. We may throw ourselves eagerly into the task of improving ourselves and reforming the world and building a great new social order. But that way, too, lies disaster sooner or later. For then we have only human resources. And they are not enough—not even the human resources of Jesus. We simply cannot carry out the great reformation, and at the same time cope with all the worries of life and the business of making a living and the whole host of competing interests and distractions that come our way. So in the end we either confine ourselves to a few minor reforms and let the rest go by the board, or else we give the whole thing up altogether. 'These are they which are sown among thistles; such as hear the word, And the cares of this world, and the deceitfulness of riches, and the lusts of other things entering in, choke the word, and it becometh unfruitful' (18-19). We need more than a Man planted firmly in our own world, more than a human Example, however heroic, if our efforts are not to be choked by all the stifling influences around us, if our Christianity is to be a thing of drive and power.

And now, if we are not to regard Jesus merely as a historical Figure, or a Divine Being, or the great Hero and Example of mankind, then there is surely only one thing left to do. And that is simply to take him for what he is: the Christ who is fully God and also fully Man, who is even now bringing and maintaining the new order of God right here on this earth. When we can take him that way, then we really begin to get somewhere. Then we have a Lord who is as alive and meaningful today as ever he was, because no time or space can ever separate us from him. Then he is not up in the air, but as close to us as any man can be; and his new order does not consist of ideals that have still to be put into practice, but it is already in practice right here and now and only waiting to be recognized. Then, too, we need not be choked and stifled by all the worries and ambitions and distractions of life, for we have a Lord who is perfectly able to cope with them for us and free us from their grip. Only when we recognize the living Christ ever present with us, fully God and fully Man—only then will our

Christianity become alive and enduring and powerful, firmly rooted in this earth, and nourished and sustained from heaven. Only then does his self-giving bear fruit and his kingdom take shape, in lives of abiding faith and hope and love.

The great difficulty here, of course, is that we cannot *see* him or his new order. But we may be quite certain that one day we shall. For he does not intend to remain hidden for ever, any more than the candle is meant to be left for ever behind the flour-bin or under the bed: he intends to be manifested for all to see when the time comes. Already, in fact, he has enacted his own parable in one way. For just as the candle may be stowed away for a time, so he himself was hidden away for years, the Carpenter of Nazareth, the Preacher and Healer of Galilee whose teaching and signs were never properly understood. But as the candle is brought out and set on the candlestick when night comes, so when the world's darkness was at its thickest he came out from his obscurity and was 'set on a stick' for all to see—and above his head for all to read the title: 'Jesus of Nazareth, the King of the Jews' (John 19.19). Probably it was written in mockery, that title. But there is many a true word spoken in jest, even in such a sarcastic jest as Pilate's. There at any rate it was, and the secret was out at last. Jesus of Nazareth—the Man they all knew. The King of the Jews, who have no real King but—God. Written, we are told, in all three great languages of the ancient world, so that everyone who saw it might understand. If they did not understand, it was not for want of telling. And it will not be for want of telling if we do not understand. *That* is who he is: Jesus of Nazareth, who lived a life as human as any other—the King of the Jews, who is God alone. And *that* is how he founds his kingdom: by letting himself be mocked and spat on, battered and crucified, in order to win the world through shame and make even the wrath of men to praise him (cf. Ps. 76.10). It may often seem to us utterly fantastic and impossible. But it is true nevertheless—as we shall see for ourselves when the time comes for him to enact his parable again in a still bigger way.

Only, let us be very careful what we make of it all meantime. We must not doubt Christ's presence just because we cannot see him, or let the hiddenness of his new order obscure its truth. We must rather make full use of the one great clue we have: that Cross with its clear superscription. It has been set before us often enough, and it provides light enough to be going on with until the time for the final great manifestation. But here again the measure of our attention decides how much we shall be given. Those who choose to ignore the Cross, or look with only half an eye, will go on from one blunder to another until they finally lose the little bit of life they have. But if we are willing to keep that Cross before us constantly until its amazing truth sinks into us, then we shall be given the faith to believe what we cannot see or even properly understand. And more than that, we shall be given a whole new life already, now.

Scene 4: *SO IS THE KINGDOM*

And he said, So is the kingdom of God, as if a man should cast seed into the ground; And should sleep, and rise night and day, and the seed should spring and grow up, he knoweth not how. For the earth bringeth forth fruit of herself; first the blade, then the ear, after that the full corn in the ear. But when the fruit is brought forth, immediately he putteth in the sickle, because the harvest is come. And he said, Whereunto shall we liken the kingdom of God? or with what comparison shall we compare it? It is like a grain of mustard seed, which, when it is sown in the earth, is less than all the seeds that be in the earth: But when it is sown, it groweth up, and becometh greater than all herbs, and shooteth out great branches; so that the fowls of the air may lodge under the shadow of it. And with many such parables spake he the word unto them, as they were able to hear it. But without a parable spake he not unto them: and when they were alone, he expounded all things to his disciples. (4.26-34)

Here are two more parables about the kingdom Jesus brings, both based on facts of everyday. The first is, that once the farmer has sown his seed, it grows in ways that are none of his doing. It grows without him, whether he wakes or sleeps. And he does not know how it grows. The whole process goes on 'by itself' (28)—or, to use Mark's own word, 'automatically'—until the corn is ripe and the farmer has harvest work to do. That is the one well-known fact. And the other is this. When you sow the tiny mustard seed, it grows into a plant that is bigger than all the rest—rather an exaggeration, we might say, but travellers tell us that the mustard plant of Palestine really does become a bush ten or twelve feet high. These, then, are two simple facts everyone knows. Jesus uses them here to set before us the mystery of his kingdom in ways we can all grasp: 'with many such parables spake he the word unto them, as they were able to hear it' (33). *Able*, yes—but are we also willing? For here again we shall understand only if we are willing to look the way they point, only if we approach them as disciples who are ready to learn their meaning from Christ.

One thing at least they cannot mean, if we approach them that way. They cannot mean that, like the seed, God's kingdom gradually grows. That was a favourite idea of our fathers fifty or a hundred years ago, and is oddly popular in some quarters still. But it is not the outlook of Christ. He never said, 'The kingdom of God is now beginning to grow'. He said, 'The kingdom of God is at your very door, so change your ways and believe this good news' (1.15). He did not tell his disciples, 'All power is gradually being given to me.' He told them, 'All power *is* given to me, so now go and live accordingly' (Matt. 28.18 ff). For Jesus the great new order of God's sovereignty is not a gradual growth which will one day be completed. It is already here. And it only remains for men to recognize it and take their place in it in faith, until the day when it will be made plain for all to see.

But the question is, How does it come? How is it to be made plain for all to see? How can we be expected to believe it, and what is our proper place in it? That is where these parables come in. They mean that the mystery of God's kingdom is like the mystery of growth: not man's work, but God's.

In the world of nature man sows and harvests, but in between it is no human power that makes the seed grow, 'of itself' (28), 'he knows not how' (27). So it is also with the new order of God's sovereignty. Jesus comes preaching and healing, sowing the word in our human world. And his word, 'automatically', bears fruit in a following of men and women with restored powers of body and mind. More than that, Jesus himself is 'cast into the ground', buried in a grave. But the third day he rises again to be what the apostle calls 'the firstfruits of them that slept' (I Cor. 15.20), and the result is a vast rich harvest of redeemed lives. That is how God's kingdom comes on earth. It is not man's doing any more than the growth of the seed is. It is the work of God's own Spirit, beyond our comprehension and beyond our control, creating anew the world he has made.

But must there not be more to it than that? Only Jesus preaching and healing, only Jesus crucified and buried—how can that alone produce a new order that embraces all mankind? Well, look at the tiny mustard seed and what comes of it: 'when it is sown, it groweth up, and becomes greater than all herbs, and shooteth out great branches; so that the fowls of the air may lodge under the shadow of it' (32). In Jesus' time the mustard seed had long been a byword for the smallest of all things. And ever since the days of Ezekiel and Daniel the tree in whose shadow the fowls of the air may dwell had been a recognized symbol for a world-wide empire embracing all peoples (Ezek. 17.22 ff; 31.6; Dan. 4.10 ff, 20 ff). But even if we did not know that, the point would still be obvious. Out of the tiny mustard seed sown in the earth God can create a bush that shelters a whole flock of birds. And when Jesus sows his words in this earth and is finally buried in it himself, then that may seem insignificant enough. But by the same power God can and does create out of it his world-wide kingdom in which all mankind can find rest.

It may seem that all that is only explaining a mystery by a mystery: to say the mystery of God's kingdom is like the mystery of growth is not much of an explanation after all, since we know as little about the one as about the other. Only, Jesus was not trying to explain, so much as to help us to *believe*. We never see a seed germinate and grow in the earth. But we know quite well it does do so. Then why not be equally sure that God's kingdom really *is* present all round us, although we cannot see it? None of us knows *how* a seed grows. But everyone knows *that* it does. And we can be just as certain that God's new order is already in operation, even if we cannot explain exactly *how* it works. No gardener in his senses goes digging up his seeds every other day to see if they are growing, and how: he simply believes they are, and believing that, he waits until he does see them. Then why should we not also believe in the divine kingdom we cannot see, and in that faith wait patiently until the day of final manifestation comes? Everyone knows for a fact that a grown plant is a much bigger thing than the seed from which it comes. How odd, then, if we find it difficult to believe that the comparatively small events of Jesus' life and death could have a result that transforms the whole world! In short, there is little enough we can see or understand about the mysterious process by which God makes things grow. But for all that we believe in it—and depend on it for the wheat that makes our daily bread. So, too, we can neither see nor trace out nor fully comprehend the working of his eternal kingdom in our midst. But is that any reason why we should not believe and hope in it, and our whole lives depend on its truth? No doubt there are flaws in that argument, if you like to set clever minds on to it and carve it up by cold logic. But as we have said before, Jesus' parables were never meant to be watertight logical arguments. We grasp them not merely with our mind, but by our attitude. And if we will take these two quite simply, as a child would take them, then we shall find them a tremendous help to our faith.

That surely is one purpose Jesus meant these parables to serve. But there is also another. They do not only help to strengthen our faith. They also put us firmly in our place. And much need too. For we are all so ready to get too big for our boots. Especially in these days when we have greatly increased the yield of the ground by our planned and mechanized farming, and our insecticides and our chemical manures, we are apt to run away with the idea that *we* are the great people in all this. But no, these parables remind us, it simply is not so. With all our discoveries and improvements, we still cannot make a seed grow, or even fathom the secret of its growth. It still grows 'automatically', we 'know not how'. Its growth is still God's work, not ours. And all we can do is to see that as far as possible our efforts should serve his purposes and not hinder them. For when the farmer forgets to marvel at God's ways and, instead of seeking to serve them, sets out to master the earth on his own, then he is heading for disaster—as we can see in the vast areas of once fertile soil which men have turned into irretrievably barren wastes.

And so it is also with the rest of life. We think too much of ourselves, not only in agriculture but all along the line. Our scientific discoveries and social welfare services have raised the standard of living to a level never known before. Our modern communications have made distance no real separation. Our international organizations are there to care for worldwide co-operation and peace. So we imagine that now, with a measure of common-sense and much give and take all round, we can soon build a great new order of mutual understanding and goodwill. We forget that the only worth-while new order does not depend on such things but on getting rid of human sin, and unless that is got rid of our great achievements will only end in the unprecedented devastation we sometimes fear. We forget that God alone can deal with human sin, as God alone can make things grow. And it is well for us that these parables should put that fairly and squarely before us. It is God who established his kingdom in Jesus Christ, long before we were born or thought of. It is God who now maintains it in our midst, while we 'sleep and rise night and day' (27). It is God who will finally bring it plainly to light, whatever we may do. From first to last it depends entirely on God, and not on our dubious achievements or decisions. That is why it is all so utterly certain and sure.

Have we, then, nothing whatever to do with it? Does it all go on far above our heads? Should our theme-song be the scathing parody:

> 'Sit down, O men of God.
> His Kingdom he will bring
> Whenever it shall suit himself.
> *You* cannot do a thing'?

No, not that either. This new order is a life of partnership between God and man—a very unequal partnership to be sure, one in which God is always the Giver and we are always only the receivers, but a partnership for all that. We are not called to found it or maintain it—that is God's work alone. But we *are* called to take our humble place in it. It is something like the partnership between God and the farmer in the natural world. No man can create a seed, and no man can make it grow. But the farmer receives the seed God has made, and plants it in the earth. Then he reaps the fruit that is produced by God's power. And just because it is *God* who is at work, the harvest is a vastly greater thing than the seed that was sown. So it is also with the kingdom. We receive the word God has spoken, and the Christ he has sent. We 'plant' them in our hearts and lives—and reap the fruits of faith and hope and love, goodness, joy and peace. We take the word God has spoken and the Christ he has sent. We plant our witness to them in the world around us—and the harvest is fellowship, understanding and brotherhood. It is all God's doing. That is why these fruits are out of all proportion to the little we have done. And yet we also have our little part to do. We cannot ourselves make God's word, or his Christ, or even a good Christian witness. Neither can we ourselves produce these amazing fruits. But we *can* 'sow' and 'reap'. We *can* 'cash in' on what God in Christ has done. That is the place which is offered us in the working of God's new order.

The only question now is, Will we accept that place or not? When Jesus speaks of 'putting in the sickle, because the harvest is come' (29), he is quoting directly from the vivid picture the prophet Joel had used to describe the judgment of the world (Joel 3.13). And ever since Joel's day, harvest had been a recognized symbol of judgment. That gives the parable a new turn. It no longer serves only to strengthen our faith, and to put us in our proper place. It also sounds an urgent note of warning. The farmer sows—and the harvest comes 'automatically'. So too, Jesus speaks his word—and by their reaction men are 'automatically' judged. Jesus gives himself to be buried in our earth and rise again —and 'automatically' men's fate is determined as they accept or reject him.

When the time is ripe, 'immediately he putteth in the sickle, because the harvest is come'. Jesus had said right at the start that with his coming the time *is* ripe, and men must therefore change their ways and believe in him. Here, in these parables, he again summons us to faith and bids us take our place in his new kingdom. And even as he speaks the sickle of judgment is at work. Will we take his words to heart and seize the opportunity he offers? Then we shall find new faith in the kingdom and new grace to take our proper place in it. Or—will we simply go our own way and pass him by? Then we shall be setting the seal to our own condemnation. God's kingdom still stands either way. Either way his sovereignty will be exercised—in redemption or in judgment. But it will make all the difference in the world to us which way. And it is for us to decide.

SCENE 5:

'HE STILLETH THE NOISE OF THE SEAS . . .'

And the same day, when the even was come, he saith unto them, Let us pass over unto the other side. And when they had sent away the multitude, they took him even as he was in the ship. And there were also with him other little ships. And there arose a great storm of wind, and the waves beat into the ship, so that it was now full. And he was in the hinder part of the ship, asleep on a pillow: and they awake him, and say unto him, Master, carest thou not that we perish? And he

arose, and rebuked the wind, and said unto the sea, Peace, be still. And
the wind ceased, and there was a great calm. And he said unto them,
Why are ye so fearful? how is it that ye have no faith? And they feared
exceedingly, and said one to another, What manner of man is this, that
even the wind and the sea obey him? (4.35-41)

'And the same day, when the even was come, Jesus saith unto
the disciples, Let us pass over unto the other side' (35). To us that
seems as harmless as suggesting a breath of air before supper. But
to the disciples it must have seemed like asking for trouble. No
wise fisherman would venture on to the Sea of Galilee in the evening if he could avoid it, much less would he try to sail across it.
For round about sundown was the time when there was most likely
to be one of those sudden dreadful storms—when without warning
a gale would come howling down one of the gorges round the lake,
and whip the water to sudden fury and make short work of anyone
sailing there. In the daytime it was not so likely—or after dark. So
the disciples might well have thought it wiser to wait a bit. They
might also have said as much—especially as they had lived on that
lake all their lives and knew its moods much better than the Carpenter of Nazareth could do. But instead they simply did as they
were told. For that is an important part of what Christian disciple-
ship means. *Jesus* is Master here. And his ways are not our ways.
He often asks us to take what seem to us unnecessary risks. But
when he does, he has his reasons. It is not for us to argue or point
out dangers. The true disciple has no real choice but to obey.
'Jesus saith unto them, Let us pass over unto the other side'—and
without more ado 'they dismissed the multitude and took him just
as he was in the ship' (36).

There were others there that evening who were not so obedient.
Some of the crowd apparently did not disperse as they were told,
but were rash enough to go 'with Jesus in other little ships' (36).
Mark says no more about these 'other little ships'. But he makes it
plain that Jesus' boat was no better off than they were: 'There
arose a great storm of wind, and the waves beat into the ship, so
that it was now full' (37), and the disciples obviously panicked as
much as anybody. It would have suited us better to hear that Peter
and his friends, knowing they were doing the Master's will, sailed
triumphantly on, while the other boats which ought to have stayed
ashore were smashed and sunk. We should have preferred that

because it would fit in so well with our own nice sense of justice. We imagine that our efforts to be good Christian people entitle us to some sort of special consideration, and therefore when trouble comes our way, we say, 'Why *me*? Why not some of those who deserve it so much more?' But Mark did not share our crude delusions about rewards and punishments, and he painted the picture as it really is. The truth is, that even Christians have plenty of trouble to face, and neither our church membership nor the most implicit obedience to Christ's commands, nor even his own presence with us will stop it coming. These men were Jesus' disciples, sailing at his command. They had him with them in the ship. But the storm broke just the same, and was just as terrifying.

In the midst of it all, we are told, Jesus 'was in the hinder part of the ship, asleep on a pillow' (38). Some regard that as a sign of his superhuman courage and iron nerve. Others think the day's teaching had left him too exhausted to notice the danger. The disciples at the time could see in it only sheer indifference. And anyone who has ever been in an even faintly similar position will understand what they felt. It is hard to have to take extra risks just because we are Christians. It is hard, too, to discover that our obedience is not rewarded by any special immunity from danger. But when the danger materializes, and we find ourselves fighting a losing battle, and Christ does not even seem to care—that is one of the hardest things of all. No wonder these disciples found it too much to accept: 'They awake him, and say unto him, Master, carest thou not that we perish?' (38).

We may wonder what they expected him to do. But what he did do was two things they certainly did not expect. First, 'He arose, and rebuked the wind, and said unto the sea, Peace, be still. And the wind ceased, and there was a great calm' (39). With that he unveils the secret of his own tranquillity. It had nothing to do with iron nerves. And it was not due to ignorance of the danger. And least of all was it because of indifference. If Jesus could sleep peacefully through the storm, it was because he knew the security of another world: the security of God's kingdom. He knew himself one with the God who created both wind and waves. He knew they could never, like the famous monster, get out of control and devour their Maker. He knew that, whether he waked or slept, they were still subject to him and could do him no real harm. Here he lets the disciples see for themselves how true that all was. And then he does the second unexpected thing: 'He said unto them,

Why are ye so fearful? how is it that ye have no faith?' (40). By that he means to make clear that the same security was available also for them. They, too, through Jesus, were one with the God who created all things. They too, were members of that everlasting kingdom that can be battered but never destroyed. If they could only have believed and grasped that, then they would neither have been so terrified of the storm, nor so resentful of Jesus for leading them into danger and then apparently doing nothing to avert it or to help them when it came.

The same faith could answer our twentieth-century fears and resentments. We have got further than the fishermen of Galilee in tracing out the laws of nature and exploiting them to our advantage. But we still have not mastered the world, and never shall. The science that has brought new blessings has brought also new dark and unspeakable dangers. And we Christians are exposed to the dangers as much as any—often more than any. But when the storms break, what we need first and foremost is not more courage and stronger nerves, not a better understanding of the world's ways, not the ability to withdraw into our own shells and let the rest go hang. What we need is the simple certainty that even in the riskiest of situations, in the worst imaginable catastrophes, in the loneliest of struggles, our Lord is still in control. We need Paul's conviction that nothing in the whole created universe can ever separate us from him. That faith, and it alone, can take the sting out of even the sorest trials and enable us to weather every storm.

If this had been a fairy tale, or a story with a moral, it would no doubt have ended with the disciples all believing and living happily ever after. And then it would have left us with half-baked ideas of what faith is, and no idea how to get it. But Mark was not romancing or moralizing. He was telling what actually happened. And what actually happened was not that the disciples now believed more firmly in providence. Instead of that, they only became more terrified than ever: 'They feared exceedingly, and said one to another, What manner of man is this, that even the wind and the sea obey him?' (41). They had been afraid of the storm, but now they were still more afraid of—God. For that is what it amounts to. They knew perfectly well that God alone can rule wind and sea with a word. And now Jesus had done it, which could only mean that with Jesus God himself was right there in their boat. That was why they were so terribly afraid.

And they were right to be. God *is* much more terrible than any storm. For a storm at worst can only kill, but God decides what happens after that. In their holy terror the disciples were nearer the truth than we are nowadays. We so readily succumb to the curious modern fallacy that the fear of God is a lot of primitive poppycock and there is really nothing in him to be afraid of. But then we are only deceiving ourselves. When the old Genesis story makes Adam say, 'I heard thy voice in the garden, and I was afraid' (Gen. 3.10), it is not speaking just for primitive man: it is expressing what lies somewhere in every guilty heart from that day to this. We do not get rid of it by overlaying it with comfortable half-truths about God's love. We only bury it deep down, where he will have to unearth it again. And he will. How *can* we be so easygoing in our thoughts of God? Do we not realize that sooner or later he will strip us of our comfortable theories and meet us face to face? At the latest he will do it on our deathbed, but he may do it before that. And when he does, we shall be as terrified as any man, primitive or not. For if we so readily go to pieces even in the storms that break on our natural lives, how shall we ever be able to stand in the far more dreadful fires of God's immediate presence?

That is where this story has so much more to tell us. It is not only the story of a storm on the Sea of Galilee. It is also the slightly veiled version of another. Through the veil shines that later storm of Holy Week, when again Jesus took these men into danger against their better judgment, and again the storm broke, and again they were terrified out of their wits. There again they seemed to be abandoned, for their Master slept—this time the sleep of death. But again Christ rose to take control, to rescue them as before, and to reproach them again for their lack of faith. This time they grasped it, and it changed their whole outlook. We hear of them after that defying both the fury of the elements and the violence of men, undismayed by hardship and even death, certain that at any time they could approach with boldness the very throne of God himself. Why? Because at last they knew and trusted the Lord who had died for them, and risen for them, and now lived for them and in them—because they knew at last that he was in complete control both of this life and of the life beyond.

Here we begin to glimpse the real meaning of Christian faith. It is not vaguely 'trusting providence': it is personal commitment to the Christ who has rescued us and will completely redeem us. This faith knows that nothing in the created universe can ever destroy us, but more than that: it knows also that the divine judgment which must fall on us has already fallen—on him. It does not only free us from our many worldly fears: it also transforms our natural craven fear of God into healthy reverence and love. This faith is the one thing that really counts in life, whether we have to face natural perils or to stand in the presence of God. And here, too, we can see how it is to be got. It is not really 'got' at all, but given. That is how it was with the first disciples: they received it from the Risen Lord. And that is how it has always been since. True faith is not so much our doing as above all the gift of the living Christ.

But what if we are not as far as that? What if we still have no faith? Or what of the days when we have lost it, and started to tremble again? Why, then surely the obvious thing is to do as the disciples did in the boat, and turn to Christ for help. They may not have done it very nicely. For it was not exactly a polished prayer or a polite request: it was more a cry of agony tinged with reproach. But he is not so fussy about the form of our prayer, so long as we do pray. And he is not asleep, though we may think he is—though for all the notice we often take of him he might as well be. In actual fact he is only waiting to be asked. At bottom it is as simple as that.

SCENE 6:

'. . . AND THE MADNESS OF THE HEATHEN'

And they came over unto the other side of the sea, into the country of the Gadarenes. And when he was come out of the ship, immediately there met him out of the tombs a man with an unclean spirit, Who had his dwelling among the tombs; and no man could bind him, no, not with chains: Because that he had been often bound with fetters and chains, and the chains had been plucked asunder by him, and the fetters broken in pieces: neither could any man tame him. And always, night and day, he was in the mountains, and in the tombs, crying, and cutting himself with stones. But when he saw Jesus afar off, he ran and worshipped him, And cried with a loud voice, and said, What have I to do with thee, Jesus, thou Son of the most high God? I adjure thee by God, that thou torment me not. For he said unto him, Come out of the man, thou unclean spirit. And he asked him, What is thy name? And he answered, saying, My name is Legion: for we are many. And he besought him much that he would not send them away out of the country. Now there was there nigh unto the mountains a great herd of swine feeding. And all the devils besought him, saying, Send us into the swine, that we may enter into them. And forthwith Jesus gave them leave. And the unclean spirits went out, and entered into the swine: and the herd ran violently down a steep place into the sea, (they were about two thousand;) and were choked in the sea. And they that fed the swine fled, and told it in the city, and in the country. And they went out to see what it was that was done. And they come to Jesus, and see him that was possessed with the devil, and had the legion, sitting, and clothed, and in his right mind: and they were afraid. And they that saw it told them how it befell to him that was possessed with the devil, and also concerning the swine. And they began to pray him to depart out of their coasts. And when he was come into the ship, he that had been possessed with the devil prayed him that he might be with him. Howbeit, Jesus suffered him not, but saith unto him, Go home to thy friends, and tell them how great things the Lord hath done for thee, and hath had compassion on thee. And he departed, and began to publish in Decapolis how great things Jesus had done for him: and all men did marvel. (5.1-20)

Many people find this one of the most puzzling and embarrassing of Mark's stories. For it speaks a language that is no longer ours, and some of its details are to say the least decidedly strange. Yet it would be a great pity if for that reason we were to ignore it and quietly turn the page. For there is a great deal more in this story than meets the eye. It is rather like the parables in the last chapter which we saw have a hidden meaning, so lightly veiled that a little care can easily discover it. Here, too, if we will take the trouble to look just a little beneath the surface, we shall discover several important things about Jesus, a thing or two about man—and something about the devil as well.

To see the first important thing the story tells us about Jesus, we must notice that it comes immediately after the Stilling of the Storm, and that the side of the lake where Jesus now landed was non-Galilean, half-heathen country. The first thing he does there— in fact, the only thing he does—is to cure a raving lunatic. You might ask what is specially significant about that. But those who know their Old Testament will soon see the point. For one of the best-known Psalms speaks of the 'God of our salvation . . .

which stilleth the noise of the seas, the noise of their waves, and the tumult of the people'—literally, 'the madness of the heathen' (Ps. 65.5, 7). And now Jesus does just that: he stills a storm at sea, and then pacifies a heathen madman. So here again the veil of the flesh wears thin, and we are allowed to see that this man Jesus is none other than the God of our salvation.

The second important thing we have here to learn about him is that this Jesus who is the God of our salvation does not only talk: he also does precisely as he says. Only a short time before he had spoken of his struggle with the forces of evil as 'binding the strong man' in order to 'spoil his goods' and free his household slaves (3.27). And now he puts it into practice. He finds a poor creature so dominated by the 'strong man' that 'no man could bind him, no, not with chains: because that he had been often bound with fetters and chains, and the chains had been plucked asunder by him, and the fetters broken in pieces: neither could any man tame him' (3-4). And at once Jesus shows himself as good as his word: the demons are mastered, the victim is released and is soon 'sitting, clothed, and in his right mind' (15). So literally does Jesus fulfil what we might have thought was only meant symbolically. And what then of all the other things he said—the salvation he offered, the new order he spoke of, his words about his constant care of us, so minute that even the very hairs of our head are numbered, and all the rest? These are not just idle words or vague promises: they are the words and promises of the Jesus who can be utterly relied on to keep what he says. So let us learn our lesson here and now, and let us never forget it when we read or hear his words. Both the words which look like only chance remarks and the promises which seem too good to be true—he fulfils them to the letter, every one.

There is also another thing this story has to tell about Jesus. It was only a fleeting visit he paid to that part of the country, and he did no more than cure that one man and return. He could have stayed longer if he had wished, in spite of the chilly reception from the man's fellow citizens. But he did not. So it looks as if he crossed the lake and weathered the storm for that purpose alone. At any rate, it shows how far he will go to help those who cannot help themselves. And that is worth stopping to think about. We have already seen how important it is to listen to Jesus with all our ears, and to recognize him for what he is. We have heard how vital it is to take the humble part that is offered us in the working of his kingdom. We have been urged to maintain the faith that alone can enable us to weather the storms of life, or if we cannot believe then at least to pray. But here was a man so utterly at the mercy of the powers of evil that he could do none of these things. And to help that one man Jesus made a special—and dangerous— journey across the lake! That, of course, is no reason for us to take our responsibilities lightly. He knows our abilities, and he will not do for us what we can do for ourselves. But if for some reason we *cannot* hear and see him properly, if we *cannot* take our place in his kingdom, if we *cannot* believe, nor even pray, then there is still hope for us. For this much is certain: that then Jesus himself will do whatever is necessary to *make* these things possible. No trouble is too much for him then, and nothing in heaven or earth will stop him.

These are some of the great things we can learn here about Jesus: he is the God of our salvation, he keeps his word down to the last detail, and he will go to any length to help the helpless. But the story also has something to tell us about man. For the madman of Gadara is with us still. Not that we have lunatics running about our cemeteries. But this one stands for all mankind. It is as if here, in Christ's presence, the dark ugly background of all human life suddenly crystallizes and we are shown men as they really are. Do we not still live amid the signs and stench of death as surely as this man who 'had his dwelling among the tombs' (3)? Are men not still possessed by an army of dark untamable powers that make them tear themselves with worse than stones? Are they not still somehow drawn to Christ while at the same time rejecting him, just as this man ran from far to worship him and yet also cried out against him (6-7)? It is small wonder if many say our world has gone mad, and there is no hope for it, and presently man will blast himself off the face of the earth.

Yes, our world *has* gone mad. But Jesus came to save a mad world. And therefore there *is* hope—hope for the world as a whole, and also for all its parts—hope for individual broken lives, for broken homes, for broken international relations. A man may be fool enough to make a complete mess of his life, but it need never be a hopeless mess. Disputes and difficulties may arise in our families, but none need cause an unhealable breach. International tension may bring us new horrors, but it can never bring the total annihilation many fear. For Jesus is still the God who has promised our salvation. He still keeps his word to the last detail. He still spares himself no trouble to do it. Therefore we may be quite certain that even in the craziest of situations there is always a solution. Christ himself will bring it. And the end will be that individuals, families, nations and the whole mad world of men will be sitting at his feet, clothed and in their right mind.

We come now to what is probably the most difficult part of the story—the strange parley between Jesus and the demons, and the loss of the swine: 'Now there was there nigh unto the mountains a great herd of swine feeding. And all the devils besought him, saying, Send us into the swine, that we may enter into them. And forthwith Jesus gave them leave. And the unclean spirits went out, and entered into the swine: and the herd ran violently down a steep place into the sea, (there were about two thousand;) and were choked in the sea' (11-13).

It is no good saying the pigs only took fright at the uproar the man was making and bolted into the sea, and then the primitive superstitious minds of the onlookers made them attribute the loss to Jesus, although there was really no connection. For that is not what Mark says, and merely gets round the difficulty by explaining it away. It is not much better to explain that Jews would find no difficulty here, because to them the pig was an unclean animal and they would consider the loss a good riddance. For Mark knew that most of his readers would be non-Jews, who would no doubt find this detail as troublesome as we do. And yet it is well he told the story as he did. For this puzzling detail stands to remind us of something in life that is equally perplexing, but also very important. And that is, that before the final redemption of our mad world, as before the final healing of the madman of Gadara, there is a period when the forces of evil are bound, but not yet banished. They cannot now destroy our lives, but they can still wreak havoc with our property. The ancient Hebrew poet knew something of that when he wrote the book of Job (cf. Job 1.12). The New Testament writers knew it too, and refer to it several times. And it is a thing we should never overlook, even if we cannot properly understand it. Still, within the limits now set him, the devil does the best he can. And it is a pretty good best, for he knows how sensitive men are to their possessions and how jealous of them.

That is how he managed to fool the rest of the Gadarenes (for the time being, at any rate). For we read that when they heard what had happened to the swine, 'they began to pray Jesus to depart out of their coasts' (17). The men of Gadara thought more of their pigs than of Christ, and for that reason allowed themselves to be separated from him. The men of today still do the same. He is welcome to give healing and help, and when things go wrong we will even beg him to do it. But let him only seem to come into conflict with our purse or our prestige, and how ready we are to show him more or less politely to the door! It is strange that men should prefer their own paltry property or position to the infinite blessings of Christ. But the devil knows it is true, and exploits our strange weakness to the full. It is only too easy for him to play upon our interest in the things we can measure and value, until we are ready to forgo the things that are really beyond all price. And it is well for us if this part of Mark's story puts us wise to the game. For then, surely, we shall not allow ourselves to be so easily duped.

Two more things the story makes clear before it ends. The one is that Jesus will not force himself on men who do not want him. He leaves Gadara when he is asked. For apparently he can afford to wait until they are in a better frame of mind. The other is, that while he is waiting, those whom he has helped have work to do. He will not suffer this man to remain happily with him, but sends him to prepare the others for his return: 'He that had been possessed with the devil prayed him that he might be with him. Howbeit Jesus suffered him not, but saith unto him, Go home to thy friends, and tell them how great things the Lord hath done for thee, and hath had compassion on thee' (18-19). And we, too, when he has helped us, are sent to bear witness of his love and compassion to those about us. For that is how our materially-minded world is to be won over and made ready to receive him after all, whatever the cost.

The man of Gadara apparently did his bit: 'He departed, and began to publish in Decapolis how great things Jesus had done for him' (20). And Mark tells later (7.31 ff) of a return to the same district and a better reception there. When Christ comes again to *our* neighbourhood, as he certainly will, will he find that because of our witness they are all waiting for him and receive him gladly?

The Religious Book Club

BULLETIN 169
NOVEMBER 1965
SCM Press Ltd
56 Bloomsbury Street
London, WC1

From the Editor's Desk

The Free Book

offered to all who enrol a new member in November or December is *The Secular City*, the new book by Professor Harvey Cox of Harvard (normally 21*s*). Dr Erik Routley wrote in his review in the *British Weekly*: 'Once again the SCM Press has published a book which nobody can afford to ignore. I have seldom handled a book which so radiantly combined passion, prophecy and constructiveness.' If you prefer it, we offer an alternative: the two new short paperbacks by Dr Paul Tournier, *Secrets* and *To Resist or to Surrender*.

The January Book

will be *The Triumph of Job* by Professor Edgar Jones of the Northern Congregational College, Manchester. This fresh study of a majestic poem shows that its theme is clearer than is usually supposed. The central subject of *Job* is the reality of religious faith, purified and triumphant after a rejection of shallow dogmas and a long struggle with the mystery of evil.

Some members of the Club will recall *Job and His Friends* by the late T. H. Robinson, our May 1954 book, but the new author has his own approach to this perennial masterpiece. As Professor William Barclay wrote in his Preface to *The Greatest Old Testament Words* by Edgar Jones (SCM Press 1964), through this scholar's exposition 'the teaching of the Old Testament will come alive and will be seen to be astonishingly relevant'.

The March book will be *Interpreting the Cross* by Max Warren.

David L. Edwards

James Leitch

was born in 1921, and educated mainly in the Latin and Greek classics at Glasgow's famous High School and University. He then worked on theology at New College, Edinburgh (B.D.), and at the University of Basel under Karl Barth and Oscar Cullmann (Dr. Theol.). His doctoral dissertation was on the theology of H. R. Mackintosh. But his interests were not solely theological! He was awarded the certificate of the Pollock Institute of Physical Education in Edinburgh. While in Basel he came to share Karl Barth's own passion for the music of Mozart – and married a Swiss wife (they now have two children).

In 1950 Dr Leitch was ordained to a Highland parish, from which he was called to the Scots Church, Rotterdam, in 1954. Eight years later he returned to Scotland as minister of the High Church, Bathgate, but in October 1964 he was back in Switzerland, as one of the three ministers of the historic Matthausgemeinde of the Evangelical Reformed Church of Basel. So far as is known, he is the first Scotsman to be called to a 'full charge' in Switzerland since John Knox's historic ministry in Geneva (1555–59). As may be gathered from this career, and from the list of important words of theology translated by Dr Leitch, he preaches and teaches as fluently in Dutch or German as in the language of *The King Comes*.

During 1966 he will be delivering the Hastie Lectures in the University of Glasgow. He is also busy translating for the SCM Press and Harpers *The Theology of Hope* by Jürgen Moltmann.

A. M. Hunter writes

Dr Hunter, Master of Christ's College and Professor of Biblical Criticism in the University of Aberdeen, is himself a highly popular author in this Club.

Over forty years ago, in the Preface to his *Romans*, Karl Barth declared that New Testament commentators had only done the prolegomena when they turned Greek into German (or English) and appended notes of a philological, historical or archaeological sort. To do these things, he said, was only to prepare the way for the task of genuine exegesis, which was the exposing of the Word in the words – since the first business of a biblical commentator is to elucidate the documents as vehicles of revelation. Everyone knows what Barth himself did. He turned a first-century letter to some Christians in Rome into a special delivery letter from God to the twentieth century.

About seven or eight years after Paul's *Romans*, and also in Rome, there appeared another book by a friend of Peter's which was destined to find a place in the New Testament canon: the gospel according to Mark. It is this book or rather its first half which has now received not dissimilar treatment (though it is incomparably easier to read!) from the man now called to minister in the Reformed Church of Basel to the 'GOM' of theology himself; and, if I am any judge, Barth will cordially approve the kind of existential *exposé* which Dr Leitch has given the earliest gospel.

The King Comes is not one more conventional commentary on Mark. What Dr Leitch has done is to produce a series of exciting expositions in which the central Figure of the gospel speaks not only to Christians in Nero's Rome but, just as truly, to Christians in the 1960s. Section by section from the banks of Jordan to the 'regions of Tyre and Sidon' Dr Leitch so expounds Mark's stories about Jesus that they come in personal terms and with personal challenges to Christ's people today, which is but another way of saying that in his pages the Jesus who nineteen long centuries ago came into Galilee announcing, 'The time is up, the Reign of God has dawned', stands forth as the Eternal Contemporary, uttering still to us his words of grace and judgment.

Dr Leitch is a learned man and an accomplished scholar. But reading his book, you might never guess it, so simple, so vivid, so direct, so *ad hominem* is his writing, like, in fact, the best preaching. Look up Act 2 Scene 1 ('So is the Kingdom') and Act 2 Scene 7 ('Believing ye shall have life'), and you will see what I mean. (As you have gathered, Dr Leitch sees Mark's story as a kind of developing drama of the inbreaking Kingdom.)

Maybe then your only complaint will be my own one, that Dr Leitch has stopped at the end of chapter 7 (just before the

3

gospel begins to gather pace for the passion); and, with this first fruits whet your appetite, you will order him back to his desk and pulpit in Basel for a like kerygmatic exposition of that supreme *Dénouement*, which meant a cross on a hill, and an empty grave, and a risen and regnant Saviour.

The New Hermeneutic

by ALAN RICHARDSON, Dean of York

I am often asked what this expression means. It is widely used today for the strenuous efforts now being made by New Testament scholars (and others) on the Continent to translate the meaning of the biblical writers into modern terms. How are we in a scientific age to apprehend the living message of the Bible? After *exegesis*, the scholarly attempt to elucidate the meaning of the biblical texts for the writers' own day, there must come the task of interpreting that meaning for our day. The old word 'hermeneutic' is now being used again precisely for this task, and its connexion with the work of the preacher is obvious. How can he put across the message of the Bible to modern hearers? The word 'hermeneutics' means the art of interpretation: in classical mythology Hermes was the messenger of the gods, and so hermeneutics is concerned with the communication of the truth about our existence.

Two of the leaders of this revived study of hermeneutics are Gerhard Ebeling of Zürich and Ernst Fuchs of Marburg. James Leitch has very ably translated several of the important essays of Ebeling in *Word and Faith* (SCM Press, 1963). Essays by Fuchs have been translated by Andrew Scobie and are published under the title *Studies of the Historical Jesus* (SCM Press, 1964). Their work is very closely connected with the parallel movement in continental theology which is known as 'the new quest of the historical Jesus'. The best introduction to this movement is to be found in the book of that title by James M. Robinson (SCM Press, 1959). It is relevant to mention here that the essay, which is generally regarded as having sparked off the 'new quest' in 1954, will be found in Ernst Käsemann's *Essays on New Testament Themes* (SCM Press, 1964).

Those who wish to learn more about the New Hermeneutic would be well advised to read the essay by James M. Robinson entitled 'Hermeneutic since Barth' in Vol. II of the series 'New Frontiers in Theology', published by Harper and Row (New York). The volume is itself entitled *The New Hermeneutic*; Vol. I in the series, *The Later Heidegger and Theology*, is also very informative, since it points out the connexion between the thought of the new movement and the older Heidegger-Bultmann type of biblical interpretation. It is at this point, indeed, that many of us in Britain would not wish to endorse uncritically some of the teaching of this important school. It tends to overemphasize the existentialist positions as being likely to be acceptable to modern men. At its most extreme it can make it appear that even God is only a linguistic event through which one man can speak the Gospel (or 'open the future' in existentialist jargon) to another. German critics, too, are often aware of this (see, for instance, H. Gollwitzer, *The Existence of God*, SCM Press, 1965, p. 177). But our hermeneutic task, of course, is not precisely that of the Germans; British folk are not steeped in existentialist concepts such as 'openness to the future', and we have to interpret the Bible in our own ways of understanding. But we can learn a great deal from continental theology about hermeneutic methods.

None of the books which have been mentioned will be found easy reading, and no one should begin to read them unless he is prepared to meet new ideas and to be challenged by them. One of the real merits of Leitch's *The King Comes* is that he practises the new hermeneutic method without expatiating upon it. He is familiar with the work of the leading continental theologians, but he does not mention them by name. Behind his interpretation there lies the long and arduous study of the means and the methods, but this is not obtruded upon the reader. And this is just what the 'hermeneut' today should do, as he strives to make clear the message of the biblical writer in the thought-forms and language of his hearers or readers.

Towards Anglican-Methodist Unity

by PETER MORGAN

The Vicar of Holy Trinity Church, Marlborough Hill, Harrow, outlines the story of an initiative in ecumenical education in Britain.

On 20th September 1965 'Towards Anglican-Methodist Unity', after a life of a little over two years, was put into cold storage. It had been brought into being for a specific purpose and that purpose having been accomplished, the TAMU Council were of the unanimous opinion that the end of a chapter in the life of TAMU had been reached, if not the end of the whole book.

'Towards Anglican-Methodist Unity' came into being in July 1963 when a group of Anglican and Methodist clergy and laity, who had been engaged in informal discussions for some months, constituted themselves as a Council. We elected the Very Rev. Robin Woods, Dean of Windsor, and the Rev. A. Kingsley Lloyd, then the President-Designate of the Methodist Conference, as Joint Chairmen. Two of the members of the original 'Conversations' Panel, the Rev. Dr Leslie Davison and the Bishop of Winchester, also joined our Council.

One consideration that greatly influenced our minds in those early days was that after the Report had been signed the 'Conversations' Panel had, of course, been disbanded. A vital day-to-day link between the Church of England and the Methodist Church was thus broken. It became apparent that no provision had been made for any official Anglican-Methodist 'Continuing Committee' to be established. After being encouraged by a number of Diocesan Bishops and Methodist leaders we therefore decided to form ourselves into an identifiable Movement.

Our first step was to draw up a Manifesto, expressing the determination of the one hundred distinguished Anglicans and Methodists who signed it to study, work, and pray for a proper understanding of the issues involved in the Anglican-Methodist unity proposals. A copy of this Manifesto was sent to every parish priest and Methodist minister in Britain. A few weeks later the Movement was officially launched at a Service of Prayer in Westminster Abbey and a Public Meeting in Westminster Central Hall, attended by about 1,200 people. Soon we were in contact with some 2,000 individuals who took the trouble to write to us and with whom we kept in touch by a periodical Newsletter.

A lot of our time was occupied in the arranging of a series of regional conferences, mostly designed for clergy and ministers, in different parts of the country, including Sheffield, Exeter, Leeds, Grantham, Bletchley, London, Shrewsbury and Newcastle. At these conferences questions were raised on every aspect of the proposals, and many doubts and anxieties were ventilated. They seem to have been very much appreciated by those who attended, and we would like to feel that they made some small contribution to the task of increasing understanding of the issues involved.

During our two years of life we entered, on a small scale, into the publishing business under the leadership of the Reverends Derek Bond, John Stacey and Dewi Morgan. Our most successful venture was the publication of 'A Simple Guide' to the Report, of which we sold some 9,000 copies. Other smaller leaflets and pamphlets were published in their tens of thousands and enjoyed a very wide circulation.

In quite a number of ways we were able to assist our two Churches to keep in step with each other. We played a part, for instance, in the drawing-up of the set of questions about the proposals that were eventually asked both in the Methodist Church and in the Church of England.

We found ourselves involved in the discussion of some of the legal and constitutional aspects of the 'Conversations' Report and were responsible for calling together an informal meeting at the office of the Church Commissioners of lawyers from both our Churches, some influential leaders from both Churches, and a group of Members of Parliament.

In a few areas local committees of TAMU emerged, the most successful of which was in London. The London Committee arranged an excellent series of talks and discussions entitled 'Let's Talk Together' in the winter of 1963–64 at Westminster Central Hall. These were attended by several hundred people.

'Towards Anglican-Methodist Unity' was also happy to be of service in various ways in the somewhat complex situation concerning Anglican-Methodist unity in Wales. A very worthwhile meeting was run by us at Shrewsbury, attended by many leading Welsh Methodists and Anglicans. As the result of this meeting four representatives from Wales were co-opted to sit on our TAMU Central Council.

Growing up in Christ

Family Life and Family Religion

FRANCES WILKINSON

This was the RBC book for September 1960. It normally costs 8s 6d. But so many clergy, ministers and other friends want to give it to young parents (perhaps at Christmas?) that while stocks last we are making copies of the normal public edition, cloth bound, available as a privilege for RBC members at 2s 6d only, post free. Here are some of the many tributes which have been paid to the book:

For many it is more difficult to have a Christian home than it is to come to church. All these problems are sensibly dealt with in this book written by the mother of four children. She writes interestingly, vividly, sympathetically and extremely practically. *Dr Coggan, Archbishop of York*

A very valuable book, whole-heartedly recommended by Mrs Geoffrey Fisher. She deals primarily with a child's first eight years. Every page shows how deeply she and her husband have thought out the implications of the Christian faith in terms that children can appreciate. *Church Times*

Parents will be everlastingly grateful. *Baptist Times*

To SCM Press Ltd, 56 Bloomsbury Street, London WC1

I declare that I am a member of the Religious Book Club.

Please send me .... copies of *Growing Up in Christ*.

I enclose a cheque/P.O. for ....
(2s 6d each, post free)

Name (IN CAPITALS)...

Address   ....

....

Printed in Great Britain by Billing and Sons Ltd., Guildford and London

SCENE 7: *BELIEVING, YE SHALL HAVE LIFE*

And when Jesus was passed over again by ship unto the other side, much people gathered unto him: and he was nigh unto the sea. And, behold, there cometh one of the rulers of the synagogue, Jairus by name; and when he saw him, he fell at his feet, And besought him greatly, saying, My little daughter lieth at the point of death: I pray thee, come and lay thy hands on her, that she may be healed; and she shall live. And Jesus went with him; and much people followed him, and thronged him.

And a certain woman, which had an issue of blood twelve years, And had suffered many things of many physicians, and had spent all that she had, and was nothing bettered, but rather grew worse, When she had heard of Jesus, came in the press behind, and touched his garment. For she said, If I may touch but his clothes, I shall be whole. And straightway the fountain of her blood was dried up; and she felt in her body that she was healed of that plague. And Jesus, immediately knowing in himself that virtue had gone out of him, turned him about in the press, and said, Who touched my clothes? And his disciples said unto him, Thou seest the multitude thronging thee, and sayest thou, Who touched me? And he looked round about to see her that had done this thing. But the woman fearing and trembling, knowing what was done in her, came and fell down before him, and told him all the truth. And he said unto her, Daughter, thy faith hath made thee whole; go in peace, and be whole of thy plague.

While he yet spake, there came from the ruler of the synagogue's house certain which said, Thy daughter is dead: why troublest thou the Master any further? As soon as Jesus heard the word that was spoken, he saith unto the ruler of the synagogue, Be not afraid, only believe. And he suffered no man to follow him, save Peter, and James, and John the brother of James. And he cometh to the house of the ruler of the synagogue, and seeth the tumult, and them that wept and wailed greatly. And when he was come in, he saith unto them, Why make ye this ado, and weep? the damsel is not dead, but sleepeth. And they laughed him to scorn. But when he had put them all out, he taketh the father and the mother of the damsel, and them that were with him, and entereth in where the damsel was lying. And he took the damsel by the hand, and said unto her, Talitha cumi; which is, being interpreted, Damsel, I say unto thee, arise. And straightway the damsel arose, and walked; for she was of the age of twelve years. And they were astonished with a great astonishment. And he charged them straitly that no man should know it; and commanded that something should be given her to eat. (5.21-43)

It is something new in Mark's narrative when 'one of the rulers of the synagogue' comes forward publicly and 'falls at Jesus' feet' (22). So far only lunatics and outcasts had done that. Now it was a high-up, a leading light of the local congregation. We can say, of course, that he only did it because he wanted help for his dying child—wanted it so desperately that he was prepared to go to any lengths of self-humiliation to get it. We can call that pure self-interest, and class him with the troublesome people who suddenly offer allegiance to Christ because they want a bed for the night, or a baptism, or a ticket for the Christmas party. But if we leave it at that, then we miss something else that is newer and more striking than the deflation of any church dignitary. And that is, that in the midst of all the man's obvious self-seeking, *Jesus* saw something else besides. We hear him later on saying, 'Be not afraid, only believe' (36), and using a form of the verb which means, 'Only keep on believing'. So he must have seen some sort of faith in Jairus right from the start—a faith, too, that was not ashamed of public acknowledgment. For him, a faith like that was enough to be going on with, whatever else might be mixed up with it. At once, we are told, 'Jesus went with him' (24). There was no indication yet of what he intended to do. But he was obviously going to help, not just to provide some new entertainment for the mob that followed.

That in itself is good news for every other Jairus. And we are all Jairuses, at least up to a point. We are all leading lights in some circle, large or small, or at any rate we all have our dignity and love to stand on it. And we are all afraid—afraid for a child, a brother, a parent. Or if not that, then afraid for a world so mortally sick that it seems at any moment some fool may unleash the end of everything. But are we one with Jairus also in the conviction that Jesus can help, and the readiness to pocket our pride and confess that faith at any cost? For that is all Jesus looks for in us. It may be with a very rickety faith that we come to him, and one that is corrupted by all kinds of base motives. But if we believe in him *at all*, and if we are ready to come off our pedestals, real or imaginary, and openly confess our faith such as it is, then Jesus will certainly go with us as he went with Jairus. And his very presence is a guarantee of help—real help. For even if we do not know what he intends to do, we may be quite sure that he does not go with us for nothing.

On the way to Jairus' house another new thing happens. Till now everyone who wanted help from Jesus had come openly to ask for it. And if even Jairus with all his influence could not get round that, then we might suppose there is no other way. But now comes a woman who tries a different approach. Like Jairus, she knew she was beyond all normal help: for twelve long years she had tried everything and only got worse. Like Jairus, she was certain Jesus could help her. But—and this is the new thing—she wanted her cure on the quiet. Perhaps she was shy and could not bear to have everyone looking at her. Or it may be she felt herself too unimportant and dared not interrupt. At any rate, she thought it was not necessary to put herself forward at all: 'she came in the press behind and touched his garment. For she said, If I may touch but his clothes, I shall be whole' (27-28). And amazingly, it worked: 'straightway . . . she felt in her body that she was healed' (29).

But still more striking than the success of this secret faith is that Jesus refused to let it rest there. He knew something had happened and stopped at once with the question, 'Who touched my clothes?' (30). It might seem to the disciples a ridiculous question when people were milling all round him. But still he kept on 'looking round about to see her that had done this thing' (32). And under that gaze she overcame the shyness or humility or whatever else it was that had made her hesitate to approach him openly in the first place. Now, with 'fear and trembling', she too 'came and fell down before him, and told him all the truth' (33). Only then were her fears set at rest and her cure made permanent: 'He said unto her, Daughter, thy faith hath made thee whole; go in peace, and be—remain—whole of thy plague' (34).

There is something important here, especially for all who try to keep their faith strictly to themselves. And there are many such. It is not always only pride that makes us hesitate to acknowledge openly our need of Christ and our confidence in him. It may be from a shyness that shrinks from any sort of limelight. It may be from a sense of inferiority, as if nothing *we* do could make much difference anyway. It may perhaps be for other reasons. At all events, here we learn that even a secret faith will do for a start, and even to it Jesus' response is immediate. But here we learn also that such a faith can *only* be a start: it must come out into the open if it is to bring lasting benefit. And part of Jesus' response is to *bring* it out. It was surely something about *him* as he stood there looking at the woman that enabled her to overcome her hesitation. And by the same power he will help us over ours. That is the second great new thing in this passage. Christ is not only quick to hear and answer any confession of faith, even a questionable one. He is also instantly aware of the secret faith even of one individual among hundreds, and part of his response to such a faith is to help it to the open acknowledgment without which it can never get us far.

But now Mark goes on to the most startling thing of all. He has tried again and again to show us that Jesus is Lord in every realm of life and his kingdom victorious over every hostile power both in the natural and in the spiritual world. He has shown us that faith alone is necessary in order to receive and appropriate the blessings of the kingdom. And now he has added that Jesus can deal also with all the inward enemies that seek to corrupt our faith, or to smother it before it can be fully expressed. These are glorious promises. But the very next sentence he writes brings us back to earth with a bang: 'While Jesus yet spake, there came from the ruler of the synagogue's house certain which said, Thy daughter is dead: why troublest thou the Master any further?' (35). *Dead*— we know what that means, and we know it will come to us all. And that rather takes the glory out of the great promises. For what real good is even the most perfect faith, and what real help are any of the blessings it brings, when at any moment death may strike and put an end to them all? It is not surprising if the prospect of death should chill our enthusiasm for the 'good fight of faith', as if it were not worth troubling ourselves or Christ for blessings which are to be short-lived after all. It would be even less surprising if Jairus had given up at this point, because for him death was not just an imminent prospect but had already struck.

Only, Jairus never got the chance to give up, because before he could do anything at all Jesus had seized hold of him and taken him off to witness a far more momentous struggle than any we have heard of yet. For Jesus does not share our belief that where there is life there is hope, but once death has spoken there is no more to be done. Jesus who has already conquered so many of man's enemies has no intention of capitulating before the last one. And still, in Mark's urgent, breathless sentences, we can sense the determination of one who has heard a challenge and is going to make no bones about answering it. 'As soon as Jesus heard the word that was spoken, he saith unto the ruler of the synagogue, Be not afraid, only believe' (36). And then he goes into action. He shakes off all unnecessary spectators, and makes straight for the home of the dead girl. There he bundles out the mourners who form the retinue of death, goes into the girl's room, takes her by the hand, bids her rise, and—at once death has to surrender its prey!

It is not just a matter of some dead girl being restored to life. It is like a flash of lightning that bursts down through our dark death-ridden world and lets us see for a moment how it really looks. It is a solemn act of protest, a first resounding blow at the whole cult of death and our universal submissiveness in face of it. Jesus cannot abide the way we take it for granted that there is no arguing with death. For him that is monstrously untrue, and a denial of all God stands for. For God has intimated time and again that the end of his ways with men is not death but life. The truth is, as Jesus says, that death is a sleep (39). And what usually follows sleep is an awakening. And here he gives a first practical sign that it is really so. There is something peculiar and high-sounding about the words as translated in our Bible: 'Damsel, I say unto thee, arise' (41). But what Jesus actually said was much more like, 'Come on, lass, time to get up'. For him the conquest of death is as natural as that—as natural as getting up in the morning.

True, it takes *Jesus* to deal with death like that. No one else would have thought of trying it, and no one else would have succeeded if he had. It is not as if there were some inevitable immortality of the human soul, or anything in us which makes our resurrection a foregone conclusion. We cannot ourselves guarantee to rise from the dead, any more than we can guarantee to wake tomorrow morning. Jesus and Jesus alone is the Vanquisher of death. As he said on another occasion, not 'There is a resurrection and a life', but '*I* am the resurrection and the life' (John 11.25). If he could deliver this girl, and if he can deliver others, then that is because in his own resurrection he conquered death once for all—for all who believe in him before or since. That is why, when he claimed to be himself the resurrection and the life, he added the promise, 'He that believeth in me, though he were dead, yet shall he live: and whosoever liveth and believeth in me shall never die.' And here, too, in the passage before us, the note of faith is emphasized. 'Be not afraid,' he said to Jairus, 'only believe' (36). Because Jairus believed, he got his daughter back. And because we, too, believe, we shall have our loved ones again, and ourselves be snatched from the hands of the death that will one day claim us.

But *do* we believe? That is the question that is put to us here. It is put in deadly earnest, for the right answer will make all the difference to our whole life. But it is not flung at us like an ultimatum. Christ does not bang the table and say, 'Believe, or be damned.' He knows what a delicate plant human faith is and how carefully it has to be handled. In the matter of faith it is specially true what Isaiah once said: 'A bruised reed shall he not break, and the smoking flax shall he not quench' (Isa. 42.3). He will accept any faith, even a very questionable one, even a secret one. He will nurse it to fullness and open confession. And if the battle should become so fierce and the strain so great that it seems our faith must crumple up altogether—why, then he will seize hold of us as he did Jairus, and say, 'Be not afraid, only believe'. He says it so persuasively, so commandingly, that like Jairus we find we have really no chance to do anything else but believe. And in that faith we shall discover not only that his mercies are new every morning of this life. We also find that in him there is life eternal for us and ours.

ACT III

The Scope of the Kingdom

SCENE 1: *HE CAME UNTO HIS OWN*

And he went out from thence, and came into his own country; and his disciples follow him. And when the sabbath day was come, he began to teach in the synagogue: and many hearing him were astonished, saying, From whence hath this man these things? and what wisdom is this which is given unto him, that even such mighty works are wrought by his hands? Is not this the carpenter, the son of Mary, the brother of James, and Joses, and of Juda, and Simon? and are not his sisters here with us? And they were offended at him. But Jesus said unto them, A prophet is not without honour, but in his own country, and among his own kin, and in his own house. And he could there do no mighty work, save that he laid his hands upon a few sick folk, and healed them. And he marvelled because of their unbelief. And he went round about the villages, teaching.

And he called unto him the twelve, and began to send them forth by two and two; and gave them power over unclean spirits; And commanded them that they should take nothing for their journey, save a staff only; no scrip, no bread, no money in their purse: But be shod with sandals; and not put on two coats. And he said unto them, In what place soever ye enter into an house, there abide till ye depart from that place. And whosoever shall not receive you, nor hear you, when ye depart thence, shake off the dust under your feet for a testimony against them. Verily I say unto you, It shall be more tolerable for Sodom and Gomorrha in the day of judgment, than for that city. And they went out, and preached that men should repent. And they cast out many devils, and anointed with oil many that were sick, and healed them. (6.1-13)

When Jesus came home to Nazareth, there were no 'Welcome Home' banners, no bands or crowds to fête the 'local boy made good'. It seems he had to wait till the sabbath service before he could find a crowd to speak to at all. And even then the majority treated him with suspicion and resentment and flat rejection. They 'were astonished, saying, From whence hath this man these things, and what wisdom is this which is given unto him . . .?' (2). It may have been only mystification—though that in itself would be enough to arouse their suspicions, for the countryman is always suspicious of what he does not understand. But no doubt there was also resentment in it—the note of 'who does he think he is, to talk to *us* like that?'—for that, too, is a typical reaction of the villager to anything that is above the average and challenges his easygoing ways. But what set the crown on their rejection was the familiarity that proverbially breeds contempt. Is he not the carpenter, whose life and background we all know? Then let him stick to his bench and not set up as an authority on religion. Is he not the son of Mary? Then let him keep to the murky background where such people belong—for to call him by his mother's name instead of his father's was to insinuate that the only real mystery about him was the mystery of a dubious birth. They knew him too well to take his claims seriously. Or they thought they did. And Jesus has to recognize that a prophet is nowhere treated with such scant respect as 'in his own country, and among his own kin, and in his own house' (4).

All that is surely a parable—a striking example of what John set in the forefront of his Gospel: 'He came unto his own, and his own received him not' (John 1.11). But the parable has still not lost its meaning. Where should Christ be more at home than in the Christian culture of our western world? But when educated people deny his Godhead or his Manhood because they cannot see how he can be both God and Man, or when they try to explain away the miracles that do not fit in with their ways of thinking and the parts of his teaching that baffle and mystify them, is that not Nazareth again, suspecting what it does not understand? When he speaks to the easy western conscience on matters like subject peoples or racial discrimination or the distribution of wealth, or when he begins to challenge some other vested interest, do men not object as hotly as they did in Nazareth, because they are still as touchy as ever, still as resentful of everything that disturbs their satisfaction with things as they are? And is it any better in the church—in the Christian congregations who of all people should be his very own? One often feels that there he is too well known. We have grown up since childhood with the picture of Jesus before us and the Gospel stories in our ears, and pride ourselves on knowing it all so well. But our very familiarity can be as great a stumbling-block as it was in Nazareth. Let him startle us with something that seems out of character—something out of keeping with the picture we have formed of him—and at once we bristle with the suspicion that this must be wrong. Let him claim a direct concern with the practical details of life, and we turn away with dark mutterings about 'politics in the pulpit', or protest that religious teachings cannot always be applied directly to the realms of science or economics or the business world.

It is rather odd that the people of Nazareth knew him as the carpenter and therefore felt he had no right to set up as an authority on religion, whereas we think of him as a religious teacher and therefore out of place in the workshop and the office and the world of practical affairs. But the result is the same: he was not wanted in Nazareth, and he is not wanted in our modern world. He is not wanted in our business conferences or our industrial disputes. He is not wanted in our national and international assemblies—except perhaps to grace them with a formal prayer at beginning and end and a few so-called 'Christian principles' in between. He is not wanted even in his own church, except as a figurehead to be worshipped on Sundays and other times of devotion and for the rest quietly ignored where he does not suit. Still 'he comes to his own, and his own receive him not'.

That is why so little that is really exciting ever happens among us. We are told that in Nazareth Jesus 'could do no mighty work' (5). He can do none here either, and for the same reason. It is not because men can somehow curtail his power, but because he will not force himself on those who do not want him. It is not surprising if our lives are then dull and dead—as it is not surprising if a man who will not connect his house to the electric cable at his door should then have to live in darkness or candlelight. What *is* surprising is the way we persist in throwing away the chances we are given. Mark says that in Nazareth Jesus 'marvelled because of their unbelief' (6). And he has as much reason now to marvel at ours. Is it not amazing, for example, that nations who want peace should still put their trust in armaments and atom bombs instead of in the only Prince of Peace? And is it not the height of foolishness that men who were made for fellowship should still believe so firmly in their own selfish interests that they will not take seriously Christ's call to the blessings of service? We should surely have learned by now that force never brings peace and self-interest

D

always creates more problems than it solves. And all the time it
could so easily be different. For Christ still comes to us. His power
to heal and bless us is still unimpaired. How truly amazing if we
should reject him just because he sometimes puzzles or disturbs us
or because sheer familiarity has dampened our expectations!

He came to his own, and they turned against him. That is one
reason why those who are still 'with him' have work to do: 'He
called unto him the twelve, and began to send them forth' (7). It
was in face of the wholesale recalcitrance of the people and their
leaders that he had first called these men 'that they should be with
him, and that he might send them forth . . .' (3.14). Now, in face
of the rejection by 'his own', he actually sends them. And in the
commission he gives them we can see his commission to the true
church in every age, to those who are 'with him' and truly 'his
own'.

He sends them out just as they are—though they were obviously
not yet completely prepared for their task and had not yet fully
grasped and understood what it was all about. They had been with
him, knew at least something of him, and were ready to stand up
for him. And that was enough for a start—as it will always be.
Those who wait till they 'know all the answers' will wait till dooms-
day.

He sends them by twos—not just because that is the regular
number of emissaries to deliver a message, but because the church
is essentially *togetherness*. Christ imposes no uniform pattern on
his servants. As individuals these men were very different, and in
some cases the difference was as extreme as it could well be. But it
was only in togetherness that they could fulfil their task. Two is the
minimum. The two may well gather more around them. But there
is no place for mere individualists here.

He sends them with 'power over unclean spirits' (7). And that
begins with emancipation from the unclean spirits in their own
hearts. He exorcises as it were the spirit of dependence on material
things: 'take no collection bag . . . and no money in your purse'
(8). He banishes the spirit of anxiety for their bodily needs: 'take
no bread . . . and no second coat' (8-9) to be a blanket for the
night if necessary. He dismisses the spirit of restlessness and indecision: 'no chopping and changing, but where you are accepted,
stay there—and where you are rejected, leave at once' (10-11). He
excludes any thought of personal gain: 'where you are not ac-

cepted, shake off the dust from your feet for a testimony to them'
(11)—a testimony, surely, that they have come to give, and where
they can give nothing they will certainly take nothing either.

He sends them with staff and sandals (8-9). Not with slippers and
dreams. For this is no fireside philosophy that is committed to
them, but a supremely practical, down-to-earth task. It means
walking the busy roads of life—the rough with the smooth, the
precarious with the easy. The staff belongs in their hand and the
sandals on their feet, and they will have much need of both.

Such is the commission he gives them. And at once we are told,
'they went' (12). And as they went, they found it worked. It was
possible to achieve something in spite of all their inexperience and
inadequacy, possible to manage without financial backing and the
assurance of bodily protection, possible to keep on without waver-
ing or swerving or letting up, possible to give without bothering
about the return. It worked, too, not only for them. They called
others also to the same change that had been wrought in them.
And men listened—not all, but many. And the many who listened
not only experienced a great change of heart, but being healed in
heart they found healing also for sick bodies and shattered nerves.
'They went out, and preached that men should repent. And they
cast out many devils, and anointed with oil many that were sick,
and healed them' (12-13).

With that it all took practical shape in these men's lives. And
now, in one form or another, it seeks to take practical shape also
in ours. Still, today, he comes to his own—to us. Shall we be
against him, like the people of Nazareth, or *with* him like the
disciples? For there is no middle way: 'he that is not with me is
against me', as he said himself on another occasion (Matt. 12.30).
To be *against* him, whatever the reason, is to bar the door to everything in life that is truly exciting and worth while ('he could there
do no mighty work'!). To be *with* him is inevitably to be sent
forth. He sends us just as we are, without more ado. Not alone,
but as members of a fellowship. Not in our own power, but in his.
And in that power there is freedom for us from the unclean spirits
that so often frustrate and stultify our lives: freedom from our
enslavement to material possessions, freedom from the tyranny of
bodies that get out of hand, freedom from the constant burden of
worry and indecision, freedom from the insidious urges of the
profit motive. Only, let us remember the staff and sandals! This

freedom is not to be had by thinking about it, or discussing it. We have to put on our shoes and take our stick in our hand, get on to our bicycle or bus or into our car, or whatever our usual means of locomotion is. We have to get out among the dirt and noise and traffic of the world, and trust him for the rest. It is only there that his power works. But there it does work, as it always has and always will. For it is the power of Jesus Christ, yesterday and today and the same for ever.

SCENE 2: *TO THE LOFTY*

And king Herod heard of him; (for his name was spread abroad:) and he said, That John the Baptist was risen from the dead, and therefore mighty works do shew forth themselves in him. Others said, That it is Elias. And others said, That it is a prophet, or as one of the prophets. But when Herod heard thereof, he said, It is John, whom I beheaded: he is risen from the dead. For Herod himself had sent forth and laid hold upon John, and bound him in prison for Herodias' sake, his brother Philip's wife: for he had married her. For John had said unto Herod, It is not lawful for thee to have thy brother's wife. Therefore Herodias had a quarrel against him, and would have killed him; but she could not: For Herod feared John, knowing that he was a just man and an holy, and observed him; and when he heard him, he did many things, and heard him gladly. And when a convenient day was come, that Herod on his birthday made a supper to his lords, high captains, and chief estates of Galilee; And when the daughter of the said Herodias came in, and danced, and pleased Herod and them that sat with him, the king said unto the damsel, Ask of me whatsoever thou wilt, and I will give it thee. And he sware unto her, Whatsoever thou shalt ask of me, I will give it thee, unto the half of my kingdom. And she went forth, and said unto her mother, What shall I ask? And she said, The head of John the Baptist. And she came in straightway with haste unto the king, and asked, saying, I will that thou give me by and by in a charger the head of John the Baptist. And the king was exceeding sorry; yet for his oath's sake, and for their sakes which sat with him, he would not reject her. And immediately the king sent an executioner, and commanded his head to be brought: and he went and beheaded him in the prison, And brought his head in a charger, and gave it to the damsel: and the damsel gave it to her mother. And when his disciples heard of it, they came and took up his corpse, and laid it in a tomb. (6.14-29)

It is often said that Mark has here done what so many people do when they begin to tell a story—got off the track and begun a long digression about John the Baptist which he had forgotten to tell at the proper time. But in actual fact it is not just a naïve digression. It is more like an interlude in some great drama. Mark uses it to fill in the interval between the sending out of the twelve and their return. And he surely means it to make plain that there are no limits to the far-reaching effects of their message. They were sent—as all Christians are sent—to call men to new life with God. They were sent with the Good News of God's new order, which knows no barriers of any kind. 'Go ye into *all* the world', Christ was to say to them later (16.15). And here already we have a foretaste of what 'all the world' means and how it is reached.

Herod might sit in his palace, far, far above the rank and file of his subjects. He was a Jew by blood, but more than half pagan by nature and could not care less about the Bible and the church. What did it matter to him, if a village carpenter turned prophet? What were twelve wandering preachers to him? Yet hardly had they begun their task than it all got to Herod's ears—and further than his ears, as we shall see. This was God's word to his world that was being proclaimed among the common people by a few faithful men. And away up in the palace 'king Herod heard' (14). For God's word to his world is addressed to all men, and God sees to it that one way or another it comes to all men. No iron curtain can stop him, and no dollar gap either. He can penetrate every social barrier, and all the many masks and pretences behind which men try to hide. And we can be utterly sure of this: The world might be full of Herods of one kind or another. There might be only one tiny group of men who are prepared to take Christ and his kingdom really seriously and try to spread his gospel faithfully. But wherever such men are to be found, it is still the same as it was then: the Herods will soon have to sit up and take notice, whoever they may be.

Yes, sit up and take notice—not just hear something that goes in one ear and out the other. What Herod heard got further than his ears, because when God's word reaches the Herods, it 'does not return to him void, but accomplishes the purpose for which he sent it' (Isa. 55.11). This is the word that 'puts down the mighty from their seats' as well as 'exalting them of low degree' (Luke 1.52). Mark has already shown us the help and healing which Jesus' gospel brings to the suffering and the down-trodden. Here he shows it bringing judgment to the high and mighty. We said a moment ago that the story is like an interlude in a drama. But it is a special kind of interlude: someone has likened it to one of Shakespeare's great soliloquies, when the stage is cleared and we are left alone with one man and his thoughts. So, too, here (although the story is told in the third person) we are given a glimpse into Herod's mind and conscience, and allowed to see the effect it all produced on him. And as we watch, we shall surely find ourselves being judged and humbled along with him. For this word brings judgment and humiliation not only to the high and mighty Herods, but also to the little would-be-greats which we all are.

What Herod hears reminds him, as the word of God so often does, of one of the black acts of his life: the murder of John the Baptist. And it calls before him one by one the events which slowly but surely led up to that crime. He remembers how John had roundly denounced his marriage with his brother's wife, how that had so infuriated Herodias that she wanted to kill John, how he had refused to allow that because he recognized that John was a good man. But in the end he compromised by arresting John and putting him in prison. Of course, he did not call it imprisonment: he called it 'observing him' (20), which means 'keeping him safe'. For in a way it was for John's own good, and he was safer in prison out of Herodias' reach. In other words, it was what we have now learned to call 'protective custody'. But Herod was not the first—or the last—to try to deal with God's claims that way. It is the simplest and commonest way really. You do not have to be a king keeping a prophet 'safe', or a dictator taking pastors into the 'protective custody' of a concentration camp. The simplest and most ordinary person can do it—can make Christianity 'safe' by confining it to Sundays only. Or perhaps to Sundays plus grace before meals or even morning and evening prayers—but at any rate confining it within certain very definite limits and not allowing it to pass beyond these limits and interfere with the rest of our lives. Which of us has never done it? Which of us is never tempted to do it? But it simply will not work. God will not be confined. And if we attempt to compromise that way, we shall only be caught out in the end and it will be made plain that at heart we were really God's enemies all along.

It need not happen at once. It didn't with Herod. He remembers

how things went quite well for a while, how he gave John a fair
amount of freedom in prison and even listened to him from time
to time. In fact he was glad to hear him, and actually 'did many of
the things' he said (20). Or as the Revised Version translates it
more accurately: 'When he heard him he was much perplexed,
and yet he heard him gladly'. Just so, we today can come to church
Sunday by Sunday to hear God's word, or can read it sometimes
in our Bibles. We can try to do many of the things he says. We can
be perplexed and disturbed by what we hear. We can even be glad
of it all—so long as we can say how much we are going to put
into practice, and when the disturbing has to stop. But no, that will
not work either. To hear God's word only when and as we will,
instead of listening on our knees whenever we are spoken to, is as
bad as to ignore it altogether. And sooner or later we shall be
shown up, like Herod, for the hypocrites we are.

Herod did not have so very long to wait. The end came, he remembers, at that fatal birthday party when nothing was further
from his mind than God and John and what he had to say. Now
he recalls it all again: his step-daughter's dancing, his delight in it,
his unthinking promise, the girl's answer—and he was cornered.
He remembers how sorry he was, but he could not break his word
—not before all his captains and officers. And so John had to be
murdered. He had not wanted that, but there it was and he could
do no more about it. 'I'm sorry, I didn't want that, I didn't mean
it to work out that way.' How often we too have echoed Herod's
words! But that does not help. That does not make us any less
responsible for the consequences of what we have done. And now
Herod had to recognize it all. He could not plead his good intentions. He could not say it was all really his wife's fault. He could
not pretend it was all force of circumstances. Now it came home
to him fairly and squarely that the whole responsibility was his,
and his alone: 'John whom *I* beheaded', he says (16)—it was *I* who
did it.

No doubt he had soon forgotten the whole thing once John was
buried. For we all have pretty short memories for misdeeds—at
least, when they are our own misdeeds. But now it was all brought
back to him by what Jesus and his disciples were doing. And as he
thought about it, he came to his own terrifying conclusion as to
what it all meant. Some might say this was the long-awaited return
of Elijah. Others might say it was one of the old prophets come to
life again, or a new prophet in his own right. But Herod was in no

doubt: it was John the Baptist, not quietly liquidated as he had thought, but returned from the dead with a new, supernatural power which this time nothing could break.

Of course, we may say that was only stupid superstition: it was not John at all, it was a different person altogether. And yet, there was a certain truth in what Herod was saying. For John had not spoken for himself, but as a prophet uttering God's word in God's name; and in Jesus we know God's word was present in human flesh. It wasn't *John* Herod had tried to 'keep safe': it was the God who spoke through him. And now the same God was getting at Herod another way. For he simply will not leave men alone, and if we slam one door, he merely opens another. Herod got rid of John—only to find a new 'John' whom he could not muzzle. And that is only a sign of what was presently to happen when the Jewish authorities murdered Jesus and put the fear of death on his disciples, but almost immediately Jesus was back again and the disciples were off through the world and the situation was a hundred times worse for the Jews than it had been before. And still there is no getting rid of Christ, no way round his claims, whatever happens to his witnesses. One may be beheaded by a tyrant, or burned by an inquisition, or shot by a dictator. One may fall a victim to—respectability or comfort or 'culture'. But God sees to it that there is always another, and another, and another. We may shut our ears to this one, and refuse to go near that one. We may build the most elaborate barricade of compromise and sham and excuse. But one day God forces his way through it all and faces us fairly and squarely with what we have done.

There Mark, surprisingly enough, breaks off the whole story. He simply shows us Herod with his fresh sense of guilt and his crude terror—and then suddenly seems to lose all further interest in him. It is rather disappointing in a way. For we should like to know what Herod did about it all. We should like to find out whether he changed his ways, or whether his fear only drove him to further excesses, and what happened to him in the end. But that would really be to miss the point. The question Mark wants to leave with us is not what Herod did about it, but what *we* now propose to do. There is so much of Herod in us all, so many things in all our lives which we should prefer to forget—not murders, but other times of compromise and weakness, times of pretence and half-heartedness, times of thoughtlessness, when our best intentions have gone all wrong. It is no use blaming someone else, or putting it all down to the circumstances, or saying we really meant well enough. Here the same word that went stabbing into Herod's heart and conscience has surely been probing its way into ours, seeking to bring home to us that excuses simply will not wash and the responsibility is entirely our own.

But now where do we go from here? There are really only two possibilities. One is to go on with the same old life, getting deeper and deeper in the mire. The other is to acknowledge our responsibility and our guilt, and cast ourselves on God's mercy in Christ. For his word is a word of mercy as well as of judgment. The judgment is necessary. It cuts, and cuts deep. But it cuts in order to heal. Herod had only got half the truth after all. He did not know that this was Jesus. He could not know that this Jesus was presently to give his own life so that all our guilt might be taken away. But we know it. And in that knowledge is our hope. Herod's story is left unfinished. And how it ended does not really matter. Our story is not finished yet either. But how it goes on matters very much indeed.

SCENE 3:

THE TWELVE AND THE FIVE THOUSAND

And the apostles gathered themselves together unto Jesus, and told him all things, both what they had done, and what they had taught. And he said unto them, Come ye yourselves apart into a desert place, and rest a while: for there were many coming and going, and they had no leisure so much as to eat. And they departed into a desert place by ship privately. And the people saw them departing, and many knew him, and ran afoot thither out of all cities, and outwent them, and came together unto him. And Jesus, when he came out, saw much people, and was moved with compassion toward them, because they were as sheep not having a shepherd: and he began to teach them many things. And when the day was now far spent, his disciples came unto him, and said, This is a desert place, and now the time is far passed: Send them away, that they may go into the country round about, and into the villages, and buy themselves bread: for they have nothing to eat. He answered and said unto them, Give ye them to eat. And they say unto him, Shall we go and buy two hundred pennyworth of bread, and give them to eat? He saith unto them, How many loaves have ye? go and see. And when they knew, they say, Five, and two fishes. And he commanded them to make all sit down by companies upon the green grass. And they sat down in ranks, by hundreds, and by fifties. And when he had taken the five loaves and the two fishes, he looked up to heaven, and blessed, and brake the loaves, and gave them to his disciples to set before them; and the two fishes divided he among them all. And they did all eat, and were filled. And they took up twelve baskets full of the fragments, and of the fishes. And they that did eat of the loaves were about five thousand men. (6.30-44)

The twelve had been sent out in pairs. But here we see that that did not mean they now became six little separate groups. It was the same work they were doing and the same Spirit inspired them, though they were working in different places and different ways. And before long it was not only a spiritual unity, but a visible one as well. For they all came together again to Jesus to tell him of their work. They 'told him everything' (30)—their successes and problems, their triumphs and mistakes, all they had done and all they had said. And they seem to have brought a lot of new enquirers with them, for we read of a great many people and much rushing about (31).

But surely such things happen still—or should do. For has our Lord not given us, too, a day—a regular day every week—when his followers can 'gather themselves together to him' (30) again like that? He means us all to be here, so that it can be *seen* how closely we all belong together; and there is something wrong if even one is missing. He means us to speak with him together about the work we were sent to do in so many different places and groups. He means us to bring as many new enquirers as we can—even if they are apt to be restless and disturb the orderliness of our service!

But now, when the disciples returned, Jesus took them apart, alone with him to rest and be refreshed. For they were being completely exhausted by their work—or rather, by the rush and disorder that are so often more exhausting than actual work. With so many people coming and going all the time they could not even manage to eat. They could not go on like that indefinitely. And he knew it. 'Come ye yourselves apart into a desert place, and rest a

while . . . And they departed into a desert place by ship privately'
(31-32).

That, too, is meant to happen still. Probably few of us would
complain of our Christian work, for quite honestly most of us
need not to rest from it but to do more! Even our daily work is not
always such a burden. For many take pleasure in it and are glad to
do it. But if ever there was a time when people were exhausted by
endless rush and bustle and disorganized comings and goings, then
it is now. That is what wears us out, for we were never made to
stand it. But Jesus made us and he knows. That is one reason—not
the only one, nor even the most important one, but *one* reason—
why he gave us our Sunday. He means us to come together here
with him and 'rest a while' in this quiet place apart.

Yet he did not take his disciples apart just to recover from it all.
It is not as if he were merely planning a sort of glorious holiday
for them as a fitting climax to a period of exhausting activity. He
only took them apart for 'a while'. And the time they were to
spend alone with him was to be a very short 'while' indeed—no
more than the hour or so which the boat took on the Lake. For
when they landed, the people were waiting for them and they were
to go on to new and stranger experiences than they had had so far.
No, when the disciples go off to rest with Jesus, that is not just the
end of a story. It is rather the beginning of a new chapter.

And again it is still the same when men come to him, or come
back to him. He does not always let us rest for long. Often enough
it is only one brief hour we are allowed to spend apart with him
before he finds us new experiences and new tasks. But after that
one hour they *will* be new. For this day is not the end of the week,
like the Jewish sabbath. It is the beginning of a new one, and sets
the tone for all that is to come. And indeed there is a new note
waiting to be sounded in our lives right now by the story that
follows. For if we can enter into it and grasp its meaning, then we
too shall find something new and exciting to challenge us, but still
more to strengthen and inspire us.

We usually call this story the miracle of the Feeding of the Five
Thousand. But that is because the feeding part is the bit that most
puzzles and perplexes us, the bit we find so striking that we overlook all the rest. In actual fact these verses tell not just of one
miracle, but of three. And the other two are really just as unlikely

as the mysterious multiplication of loaves. But there is no use trying to puzzle out what exactly happened and how. There is still less use in simply saying that it never could have happened and is all an exaggeration or a fairy tale. We know quite well that five loaves among five thousand does *not* give one each and five baskets of leavings. It simply does not happen ever, and it is not surprising if we find it difficult to believe it ever did. But the whole point is not what we men or our cleverest professors could conceivably do, not what our mathematics and the so-called 'laws of nature' will allow. The whole point is what *Christ* can do and what happens when *he* gets going with his new order. These verses do not stand in a students' textbook, but are part of the gospel—the Good News of the kingdom. They are *news*—things that never occurred before and do not fit in with what we are accustomed to. They are *good* news, because they come to make us lift up our heads and realize life is far more wonderful than we ever imagined it could be. We completely miss all that if we try to explain these miracles here, or to explain them away. It is far better to take them just as they stand, however much they baffle us, and to let them give us the new courage and hope they are meant to bring.

There is first of all the miracle of five thousand tough, able-bodied men (they must have been tough and able-bodied if they could run round the bay faster than a boat could cross it) going to all that bother to get to Jesus, and ready to listen to a sermon that lasted all afternoon. These are not the types who bother at all about religion as a rule, and they would certainly never find a sermon too short. Yet there they were, and to be quite candid our imagination boggles at the picture. We should be mighty surprised if we found a mob like that outside the church today, waiting to keep us off our Sunday dinner and clamouring to be told all about what we had learned here. But that is the sort of thing that happens when Jesus gets going. It could very well happen still. Perhaps our surprise is just the trouble; perhaps it is our very lack of expectancy that blinds us to what the eye of faith would find quite possible and even likely. At all events, in the light of this story we have every reason to believe that before we have gone very far from church today, we shall find men waiting for us. If not five thousand, then five, or fifteen—enough at any rate to stretch and challenge us. Surprising or not, they will be there—so we had best keep a look-out for them. Surprising or not, they will listen to us—so we have no need to be shy and apologetic.

And surprising or not, we shall have something to give them. For that is the second miracle: the miracle of the disciples. No doubt it was natural enough that the disciples should notice the men's need for food and should take the problem to Jesus. It was certainly even more natural that they should be taken aback by Jesus' suggestion that *they* should deal with it. At a quick estimate it would require fully two hundred pence to provide the needful— and since a penny a day was the standard labourer's wage, that means (allowing for sabbaths and festivals) virtually a whole year's wages. Well, if such a thing was obviously beyond them, what had they? Let them give that—all of it. And that is the miracle of the disciples: that they apparently had no hesitation in giving *all* they had—that they did not say they needed at least four loaves for themselves but the people were welcome to the fifth.

It is on the same conditions that we shall have something worth giving to those who will be waiting for us after church today or this week. The first thing (and unfortunately it can no longer be taken for granted even among Christians, if it ever could be) is to have an open eye for these people's needs. They may be material (have you ever noticed the inevitable gaps in our welfare services, or realized how many for one reason or another are still not covered by them?). They may be what for want of a better word we may call psychological (there can seldom have been so many nervous disorders among us as there are today). They may be, and certainly also are, spiritual. But whatever kind the needs may be, the first thing for us is to open our eyes to them. And the second thing is then to bring them to Christ in prayer. The third thing is to measure the resources we have for answering our own prayer. These of course will be absurdly inadequate. A whole year's salary would not suffice, nor would the fruits of ten years' study and spiritual discipline. But what, then, do we have? Let us count it up, and give it—*all*. To be sure, it will take a miracle to achieve that. But the miracle is possible. That is the second promise of this story.

And the third promise is, that however much or little our all may be, it will in fact be enough: 'when he had taken the five loaves and the two fishes, he looked up to heaven, and blessed, and gave them to his disciples to set before them; and the two fishes divided he among them all. And they did all eat, and were filled' (41-42). We have no means of knowing how that happened. But our best approach to it is to see it, whatever way it happened, as an acted parable. Long ago Jesus had told the parable of the Sower to illustrate how the word may often be wrongly received, but will very certainly also be rightly received and will then bear rich fruit (4.14 ff). He had gone on to say that the increase, like the growth of the seed, will be God's doing not ours (4.26 ff). And he had added that for that very reason the end result will be out of all proportion to the humble beginnings, as the mustard bush is out of all proportion to the tiny seed from which it springs (4.31 f). Now he confirms all this teaching in action—and action, too, which shows it applies not only to spiritual things like the word, but to our material things as well. They too can easily be misused and fruitlessly consumed. But when they are rightly used—when they are offered to Christ and blessed by him—they can stretch to surprising lengths and do surprising things. The story of the loaves and fishes is a most striking example of that. But it is not the only one. In one form or another the same thing could happen still, and indeed it surely will. Never fear: the little we can offer—whether in qualities of mind and heart or in outward and visible things—is a little that he can use to tremendous purpose and can turn to vastly greater account than we ever think.

Yet in the end this story has more to do than merely point the moral that with Christ's blessing a little can go a long way. It points us also to one particular 'little' that goes an infinite way. We cannot read it without thinking inevitably of *the* Bread broken for us all. Indeed, so many of the details—even to the time of year, which must have been the passover season if the grass was green as Mark says (39)—make the whole thing look as if it were in some sort a deliberate prefiguration of the first Lord's Supper. At all events there is a direct line that leads our thoughts from the five broken loaves that suffice for five thousand men to the one broken Body that suffices for all men. The miracle of the loaves is an early pointer to this greatest of all miracles—as the Lord's Supper is a sign and seal of it still. And so its ultimate message is to reiterate the promise that the death of Christ avails for each one of us. In him and through him there is enough and to spare for all men's needs both in body and in soul. It was to assure us and reassure us of that that he brought us here apart with him today. It is with that assurance that he now sends us to offer our whole selves in the service of those who will be waiting for us outside.

Scene 4: *TO THE TROUBLED*

And straightway he constrained his disciples to get into the ship, and to go to the other side before unto Bethsaida, while he sent away the people. And when he had sent them away, he departed into a mountain to pray. And when even was come, the ship was in the midst of the sea, and he alone on the land. And he saw them toiling in rowing; for the wind was contrary unto them: and about the fourth watch of the night he cometh unto them, walking upon the sea, and would have passed by them. But when they saw him walking upon the sea, they supposed it had been a spirit, and cried out: For they all saw him, and were troubled. And immediately he talked with them, and saith unto them, Be of good cheer: it is I; be not afraid. And he went up unto them into the ship; and the wind ceased: and they were sore amazed in themselves beyond measure, and wondered. For they considered not the miracle of the loaves: for their heart was hardened.

And when they had passed over, they came into the land of Gennesaret, and drew to the shore. And when they were come out of the ship, straightway they knew him, And ran through that whole region round about, and began to carry about in beds those that were sick, where they heard he was. And whithersoever he entered, into villages, or cities, or country, they laid the sick in the streets, and besought him that they might touch if it were but the border of his garment: and as many as touched him were made whole. (6.45-56)

Jesus is Lord over all, and there is no limit to his sway. That is still the message of these verses. He is Lord of men: that is why the disciples sail off alone when he bids them, and the masses disperse at his word, although no one would likely *want* to leave him after what had happened. He is Lord of nature, so that the sea provides a path for his feet and the wind falls silent in his presence. He is Lord over everything that can afflict mankind in body or soul, and therefore at his touch the suffering are not just helped but made *whole*.

Yet that does not mean that life under his new régime is all plain sailing. It never was, not even for the first disciples. They had just experienced the thrill and fellowship of a first extraordinary Lord's Supper. But now we find them toiling against a contrary wind—alone. That is nothing unusual for God's servants. How often we hear them in the Old Testament not singing songs of wonder and praise but crying out in desperation and loneliness!

How often we too have to share the same sort of experience. We all
know these occasions when we have to turn from the fellowship of
the Lord's Table to face the strain and stress of life alone—these
Mondays when the sermon that was perhaps so inspiring seems to
belong to a totally different world—these times when the presence
of Christ is only a memory and we are left to ourselves and nothing
goes right. Here is good news for such times.

The first part of this good news is, that such things do not happen by accident. The disciples did not merely drift away from Jesus.
He *sent* them away: 'He *constrained* his disciples to get into the
ship, and to go to the other side before unto Bethsaida' (45). And
if they then had to struggle on by themselves for a while, it was
not because he did not know what was happening: he saw their
difficulty in the evening already, although he did not go to them
until 'the fourth watch' (48), between three and six in the morning.

In other words, Jesus deliberately sends us off to meet with
difficulties, and deliberately leaves us in the dark alone with them.
Perhaps because there are some things we only recognize properly
that way. It has to be dark in the cinema if the picture on the
screen is to be seen clearly. So too, it may be in the darkness of
loneliness and failure that we best learn what a difference Jesus
makes. When he is always with us, we soon take it for granted
that he always will be. And when he blesses our work, we are too
ready to take the credit to ourselves. But taking things for granted
is the arch-enemy of love, as self-confidence is the arch-enemy of
faith. And we usually have to be broken of them the hard way. My
father sometimes used to warn us as children that if his precepts
would not go in by our ears, he would have to put them in by our
sterns. But in some things we are children all our lives. We have
been told repeatedly that Christ's blessings are not to be taken for
granted, and that without him we can do nothing. But it seldom
gets in through our ears, and therefore we have to learn it by pain-
ful experience. That is why Jesus often sends us off on our own and
then leaves us to toil without success. Only, we are likely to miss
the lesson after all, if we then imagine we are suffering from some
mischance that has nothing to do with him. Therefore it is well for
us to discover from these verses that in fact it is no mischance, but
a deliberate part of his training.

The second part of the good news in this passage is, that
although *we* may be in darkness and distress, *Christ* is still in

complete control. He had once likened his kingdom to the growth of the seed that goes on whether men sleep or rise (4.26 ff). Here we see a practical example of that. The disciples were—literally—all at sea and making no headway against the wind, but Jesus' sovereignty was still unimpaired. He saw them, although they could not see him. He was praying, Mark says (46), and we may be sure that he was praying among other things also for them, and they were upheld by that prayer even if they did not know it. Everything was still in order for all their temporary disorder.

And is it otherwise today? We are as much at sea as ever, and few would claim to be making real progress. A lady once lamented that with all her efforts to be a good Christian she found herself no better than she had been thirty years ago. And a minister was recently heard to confess that after forty years in the ministry he was more convinced than ever that he was neither a preacher nor a good pastor. These are two outstanding Christians, and what they said was neither false modesty nor defeatism: it was the simple recognition that, as far as we are concerned, the best of us are no better off than the disciples on the Lake, rowing for all they were worth and getting nowhere. If that were all that is to be said, it would certainly be a poor outlook for Christ's kingdom and we might as well pack up right now. But it is not all that is to be said. It is not even the most important thing. For what really counts here is, that Christ is still watching—no longer from a hill-side from which he can see only a handful of men, but from his place at God's right hand where all things are open to his eyes. And there he is not only watching but praying—praying also *for us*. Whatever else is meant by the doctrine of Christ's continual intercession for us at God's right hand, it means at least this: he is not an idle onlooker in some distant heaven, but one who actively watches over us and calls out the whole resources of God to uphold and guard us. If it were not so, we'd not be struggling on at all, for we'd have gone under long ago. Even if we do not know it, his prayer for us is still a secret source of strength. But it will make all the difference to us if we do know it. When a lone soldier or a lone group is caught up in a hot spot in the battle and faced by overwhelming odds, then resistance may seem futile. But if the message gets through to them that their commanding officer knows the position and has made arrangements for their relief, then they will hold out with new confidence and new determination. And that is the message of these verses, as of many other passages in

the Bible. Even when everything is against us, and we are making
no progress, or even losing ground, *Christ* still watches and prays.
Under his watchful eye the situation is still in control, and thanks
to his intercession we have the help and defence of God himself. If
we can only grasp that, then we can hold out, however hard the
going.

But that is not all. For there is still a third part to the good news
these verses bring for the distressed. And that is, that Jesus does
not expect his servants to go on holding out for ever with only his
watchfulness and prayer for their support. He soon comes to help
them in person: 'about the fourth watch of the night he cometh
unto them, walking upon the sea' (48). And again it is still the
same. The stormy water could not keep him from his disciples then,
and far less can anything bar his way to us now. Where Christ is
concerned, there are no impossibilities, neither physical nor
spiritual. Whatever the nature of the distress that tries us, still
through and over it all he comes to us to help and save. He comes
in his own time, and we cannot know whether that will be midnight or three or six or when it will be. He comes in his own way,
and it is not for us to say whether it is to be a spectacular way or
an unassuming one. But in his own time and his own way, he does
come.

Only, we shall have to be sure it is the real Jesus. The disciples
thought at first it was a ghost, and were more terrified than ever.
He had to speak to reassure them it was really himself. He had to
go right into the ship beside them. Only then were their fears put
to rest and their time of loneliness and testing at an end. And our
help, too, is only in him, not in one of the ghost Christs that we
have thought out or conjured up for ourselves. Not just the Hero
and Example of mankind, nor the fairy-godmother Christ who will
one day fulfil our dearest dreams. Not the great Moral Reformer,
nor the gentle Jesus who gives nice religious feelings and makes no
real claims on conduct. Not the Christ of western culture and
Opiate of the people, nor the Champion of the oppressed and
first socialist Revolutionary. Where such Christs and others like
them are at work, we have as much cause for alarm as the disciples
would have had if it had been only the ghost of Jesus they saw on
the lake. For when such Christs are followed it only makes matters
a thousand times worse. Only the real Christ can help. And that is
the Son of God who comes right down beside us in human flesh,
the Christ who speaks in the Bible and who through it still speaks

his own word of assurance to us: 'Be of good cheer: it is I; be not afraid' (50). When *he* comes to us, then there is light in our darkness and peace for our distress. And he does come. He has done it repeatedly before. And we may be certain that sooner or later he will do it again.

That is the good news this passage brings. And now, as often happens, it contains also a tail-piece, and the tail-piece points another problem. There is nothing problematical about the message itself, or about the difference it must make when it gets home to us. If we know that our various trials are neither fate nor chance but a deliberate part of Christ's purpose for us, then we can bear them patiently, without either resignation or bitterness. If we know of Christ's supreme control and his watchfulness and prayer for us, then we can hold out resolutely without anxiety or despair. If we know that presently he will come to deliver us, then we can endure not just with vague hopes that one day perhaps things may change for the better, but in confident expectation of his coming. It was because Paul knew of these things that he could speak of being 'troubled on every side yet not distressed, perplexed but not in despair, persecuted but not forsaken, knocked down but never knocked out' (II Cor. 4.8 f). The trouble with us is that we do not know it. We may assent to the message and agree in theory that it is true. But somehow it does not bite. It does not get home to us in such a way that we reckon seriously with it in practice and find ourselves upheld and strengthened by its truth. That is where the tail-piece to this story comes in.

It did not get home to the first disciples yet, either. Instead of grasping the real meaning of what had happened, they were only 'sore amazed in themselves beyond measure, and wondered' (51). Why were they so frightfully perturbed? Why did they still not understand? Because, says Mark, 'their hearts were hardened' (52) —or as the New English Bible translates it, 'their minds were closed'. Looking back, we are apt to think they must have been almost incredibly obtuse. But in actual fact we are all as bad and worse. In actual fact we have had better chances than they had had at that point. For we have followed the whole story through to the Cross itself and the day when he returned to them over the sea of death. But even with that, and with the testimony of two thousand years of Christian experience behind us, we still live as if it all meant nothing at all. Especially in our times of distress and anxiety we become so wrapped up in ourselves and our troubles that nothing else gets through to us at all.

The reason is still the same. And the remedy is still the same. There is only one who can deal adequately with minds as closed as ours. And now Mark points us back to him again in the end: 'When they came ashore, at once he was recognized. And the people scoured the whole countryside and began bringing the sick on stretchers wherever they heard he was. And wherever he went, to farmsteads, or villages, or towns, they laid the sick in the streets, and begged him that they might touch if it were but the hem of his cloak; and as many as touched him were made whole' (54-56). And once again it is the same today as always. He and he alone can give complete wholeness of body and soul. He and he alone can open closed hearts and minds and bring his message home. Everywhere, and always. The 'hem of his cloak' is enough. And there are two things worth noting about the hem of his cloak. It is so near the ground that it can be reached only by those who are willing to stoop. And it is so near the ground that it can be reached even by those who can only crawl.

Scene 5: *THE OPEN DOOR*

Then came together unto him the Pharisees, and certain of the scribes, which came from Jerusalem. And when they saw some of his disciples eat bread with defiled, that is to say, with unwashen, hands, they found fault. For the Pharisees, and all the Jews, except they wash their hands oft, eat not, holding the tradition of the elders. And when they come from the market, except they wash, they eat not. And many other things there be, which they have received to hold, as the washing of cups, and pots, brasen vessels, and of tables. Then the Pharisees and scribes asked him, Why walk not thy disciples according to the tradition of the elders, but eat bread with unwashen hands? He answered and said unto them, Well hath Esaias prophesied of you hypocrites, as it is written, This people honoureth me with their lips, but their heart is far from me. Howbeit in vain do they worship me, teaching for doctrines the commandments of men. For laying aside the commandment of God, ye hold the tradition of men, as the washing of pots and cups: and many other such like things ye do. And he said unto them, Full well ye reject the commandment of God, that ye may keep your own tradition. For Moses said, Honour thy father and thy mother; and,

Whoso curseth father or mother, let him die the death: But ye say, If a man shall say to his father or mother, It is Corban, that is to say, a gift, by whatsoever thou mightest be profited by me; he shall be free. And ye suffer him no more to do ought for his father or his mother; Making the word of God of none effect through your tradition, which ye have delivered: and many such like things do ye. And when he had called all the people unto him, he said unto them, Hearken unto me every one of you, and understand: There is nothing from without a man, that entering into him can defile him: but the things which come out of him, those are they that defile the man. If any man have ears to hear, let him hear. And when he was entered into the house from the people, his disciples asked him concerning the parable. And he saith unto them, Are ye so without understanding also? Do ye not perceive, that whatsoever thing from without entereth into the man, it cannot defile him; Because it entereth not into his heart, but into the belly, and goeth out into the draught, purging all meats? And he said, That which cometh out of the man, that defileth the man. For from within, out of the heart of men, proceed evil thoughts, adulteries, fornications, murders, Thefts, covetousness, wickedness, deceit, lasciviousness, an evil eye, blasphemy, pride, foolishness: All these evil things come from within, and defile the man. (7.1-23)

Here Jesus' old enemies the Pharisees come back to renew their quarrel. But their opposition only serves to bring out the more clearly still other aspects of the new kingdom. For Jesus' answer to them unlocks a long-closed door—a door that indeed opens 'into all the world', for through it we are given to see how all-embracing is his new order and how deep it goes.

These Pharisees had noticed some of the disciples eating bread without first washing their hands. And they objected to that, because to wash your hands before eating was a thing they were frightfully particular about. A very good thing too, we may say, for it is one of the elementary rules of hygiene. Only, for them it was not a question of hygiene at all, but of religious tradition. The washing was a solemn religious ritual. Behind it there lay the age-old question: How can man serve the holy God?—and the equally well-known answer: By separating himself from everything that is unholy. All kinds of people have believed that, and most religions have their purification rites. But the Pharisees took it all so very seriously. They wanted the *whole* of life consecrated to the holy God. And so through the years they had worked out a great tradition of ritual purifications against the many polluting influences of every day (3-4). They could not touch the food which was God's gift, without a ceremonial washing of the hands which might have touched something unholy a moment before. When they came home from rubbing shoulders with the impure and the heathen in the streets, there was another bathing ritual to go through. There was also a regular ceremony for the purification of their dishes and cooking utensils and tables. And there was a whole string of other similar traditions. You might think it all very superficial. But of course they knew it was not just the act of washing that mattered. The outward rites were the symbol of their deep desire to keep every smallest part of life consecrated to God. The very name 'Pharisees' means 'separated ones'. The whole foundation of their tradition and their lives was simply their desire to separate themselves from all unholy people and things. There, at least, we must surely confess to a great deal of sympathy with their attitude. And yet, it was precisely there that they were so utterly wrong.

That is why Jesus does not give a direct answer to their question. Instead, he goes right to the heart of the matter. He tells them their whole elaborate system was one giant hypocrisy. He did not mean they were patently dishonest and insincere. That is a sense the word 'hypocrisy' has now come to bear, but at that time it was the ordinary word for 'play-acting'. And what Jesus meant was that their whole religion was as unreal as a play. It was no more true religion than a play is real life. It was only a shadow, only an empty shell. It fitted exactly Isaiah's description of the religion of his day—full of religiosity but empty of reality (Isa. 29.13). And why? Why was their religion that looked so well really only an elaborate sham? Isaiah knew the answer to that too: because it was 'teaching for doctrines the commandments of men'—because it was all built up on their own human ideas of how God should be served, without ever stopping to ask what sort of service God himself wants. And their own ideas of how God should be served contained at least two colossal errors right from the start. Very attractive errors they are, too, and all too easy to fall into. A great many people besides the Pharisees have made the same terrible mistakes, both before and since. And if *we* are to avoid them, then we shall do well to keep our eyes and ears wide open as Jesus lays them bare.

The Pharisees, like so many before and after them, got their religion all wrong because its keynote was separation. That was to disregard God's will at the very start, because whatever else God wants of us, he wants not separation but *fellowship*. We can see that already in the Ten Commandments. There is no change of tone, no descending to something less important, when we pass from the four on the service of God to the fifth which says: 'Honour thy father and thy mother'. For it is only in fellowship that God can be served, and the smallest and most obvious unit of fellowship is the family. That was a thing the Pharisees could not see. They drove a wedge between duty to God and duty to man, and imagined God could be served at the expense of our fellow men. So it was not long before they were laying down that if a man consecrated his money to God's service then he need no longer support his parents when they were in need (11-12). And that was only one of 'many such like things' they did (13). They also objected, for example, to healing on the sabbath, because that day was set apart for the service of God alone. And in the parable of the Good Samaritan no doubt one reason why the priest and the Levite kept clear of the injured man was that if he died on their hands they would be polluted and unable to take their part in the Temple service to which they were going.

But Jesus roundly rejects an attitude of that sort. 'Thou shalt love the Lord thy God with all thy heart . . . and thou shalt love thy neighbour as thyself' (Matt. 22.37-39). And there can be no real competition between the two. For God does not want us all on our own, whatever we may be. No, 'if thou bring thy gift to the altar, and there rememberest that thy brother hath ought against thee, leave there thy gift before the altar, and go thy way; first be reconciled to thy brother, and then come and offer thy gift' (Matt. 5.23). Or if it is not our brother, then it will be our father or mother, our husband, our wife, our next-door neighbour, our workmate. . . . Christ does not offer us here a ready solution to the problem of human relationships. He does not mean that the reconciliation will be easy, or that the fellowship can be maintained without the risk of our getting hurt and soiled. But he does block the easy way out—the way that seeks to wash our hands of the others and keep our own selves right with God. No, his kingdom is for *all* men. He wants us all, in one great family—Gentiles as well as Jews, black and white, high and low, good, bad and indifferent. The door to a vast new world begins to open here. Of course, we must be ready to go through the door. We must be so set on serving Christ that we will spare no effort to foster the fellowship in which alone he wants to be served. And that means we must learn among other things to suffer fools gladly, as he does. For if we prefer, like the Pharisees, to leave the difficult people aside, if all we want is to keep our own hands clean, then we may be sure of one thing at least: we may get the most wonderful kick out of our religion, but it will all be empty and futile.

That was the one great mistake of the Pharisees. They did not understand that although it may be difficult to serve God in company with our fellow men, it is quite impossible to serve him without them. And their other great mistake was this: they forgot that no amount of separation from the unholy people and things around us can make us holy. For the source of pollution is not outside at all: 'There is nothing from without a man, that entering into him can defile him: but the things which come out of him, those are they that defile the man' (15). When the disciples asked him for an explanation, he said it is a question of the *heart*. Food cannot defile, *because it does not affect the heart*, but all that is useless or harmful is purged away by the ordinary process of digestion. It is 'from within, out of the heart' (21) that real defilement comes. Only, let us be careful what we make of that. It was not for nothing that Jesus urged his hearers to listen carefully and understand (16). For it is easy enough to misunderstand. He did *not* mean, for example, what many of us would like him to have meant: he did *not* mean that outward things do not matter, and true religion is to withdraw from them and cultivate an 'inner life' of the heart. No, he knew very well that our outward lives *do* matter. He knew too that they are full of evil things. But he meant that these evil things are the outward signs of sickness deeper down. Our hearts are evil; that is why there is evil in our lives.

That was a nasty blow to the Pharisees, who imagined that they at least were all right, if only they could keep clear of the poisonous influences around them. No, says Jesus, you can withdraw into your shell, and you can wash your hands all day, yet still have an evil mind and a poisonous tongue, because *the* great source of evil is your own heart. It is a nasty blow also to us with our modern belief in some sort of inborn human goodness that only needs to be trained up and strengthened against the evils of society and environment. No, says Jesus, there is no such inborn goodness either in your heart or in anyone else's. Only look at the things you do and think and say. It need not be adultery, fornica-

tion, murder and theft. But there are other things he obviously
finds just as bad, for he mentions them all in the same breath (21-
22). What about unclean thoughts? What about the profit motive,
and bits of sharp practice? What about being two-faced, or easy-
going? What about grudges, loose talk, feeling superior, or not
stopping to think? These things do not just come from society or
environment. Our whole heart is sick, and desperately needs to be
renewed.

Christ is here trying to open our eyes not only to the breadth of
the new order, but also to its depth. It has a wide sweep that includes all our fellow men. It also goes deep enough to penetrate
the darkest depths of our hearts. We do not always like to recognize these things. One could fill a book with the reasons we think
up for by-passing our fellows with a 'good conscience'. And one
could fill another with the arguments by which we try to rescue
our self-respect and show that there is some good in us after all.
But it is no use. Christ will have none of it. He insists that there
can be no merely private link with God, but we can only serve him
properly along with our fellows. He is equally insistent that what
we need is not a better heart, but a new one altogether.

We must face up to that fairly and squarely. Yet it is not meant
to crush us or to make us cringe. For there was a third point in
Jesus' sermon that day. It was given already in the Isaiah passage
from which he took his text. And though it may escape our notice,
it should have been obvious to the hearers, who knew their Bibles
so much better than we do. They must surely have remembered
that God's message to Isaiah was neither a demand nor a threat,
but a promise. He did not say merely: 'This people honours me
with their lips, but their heart is far from me and their religion
built up on their own human ideas.' He said: Because that is so,
'therefore, behold, *I* will proceed to do a marvellous work among
this people'. God himself will bring in a new order which will
utterly supersede the cleverest human ideas—a new order in which
perverse hearts will be remoulded like clay, and the people which
has so long been deaf to God's word will be enabled to hear it as
one family and understand (Isa. 29.13-24).

And now comes Jesus, calling 'all the people' and bidding them
'hearken unto me every one of you, and understand' (14). Now, if
we care to draw the obvious conclusion, the promise has been
fulfilled. Christ has not waited for us to put our relationships in

order or to change our own hearts. He has come himself to open
for us the way to our fellow men. He has come himself to give us
the new hearts we need. To believe in Christ is to believe that there
is a way, not just to an airy 'brotherhood of man', but to all who
are round about us now. And then we shall seek more and more to
find the way to them, even to the difficult ones—yes, especially to
them. To believe in Christ is to believe that there *is* a new heart and
a new life available for us. And then we shall strive more and more
to *live* the life of the new order to which we belong. We may
stumble again and again as we try to follow Christ into true fellowship with our family, our neighbour and all the rest. But in faith
we still go on. We may repeatedly lose our hold of the new heart
and the new life he offers. But in faith we stretch out and grasp
them again. We may manage little more than to make a beginning,
or a constant series of new beginnings. But here especially, the beginning is half the battle. Here especially, 'something attempted is
something done'.

Scene 6: *THROUGH THE DOOR*

And from thence he arose, and went into the borders of Tyre and
Sidon, and entered into an house, and would have no man know it:
but he could not be hid. For a certain woman, whose young daughter
had an unclean spirit, heard of him, and came and fell at his feet: The
woman was a Greek, a Syrophenician by nation; and she besought him
that he would cast forth the devil out of her daughter. But Jesus said
unto her, Let the children first be filled: for it is not meet to take the
children's bread, and to cast it unto the dogs. And she answered and
said unto him, Yes, Lord: yet the dogs under the table eat of the
children's crumbs. And he said unto her, For this saying go thy way;
the devil is gone out of thy daughter. And when she was come to her
house, she found the devil gone out, and her daughter laid upon the
bed.
  And again, departing from the coasts of Tyre and Sidon, he came
unto the sea of Galilee, through the midst of the coasts of Decapolis.
And they bring unto him one that was deaf, and had an impediment in
his speech; and they beseech him to put his hand upon him. And he
took him aside from the multitude, and put his fingers into his ears, and
he spit, and touched his tongue; And looking up to heaven, he sighed,
and saith unto him, Ephphatha, that is, Be opened. And straightway

his ears were opened, and the string of his tongue was loosed, and he spake plain. And he charged them that they should tell no man: but the more he charged them, so much the more a great deal they published it; And were beyond measure astonished, saying, He hath done all things well: he maketh both the deaf to hear, and the dumb to speak. (7.24-37)

In the Fourth Gospel we often find an account of some great act of Jesus, followed by a discourse which brings out its meaning. In this seventh chapter Mark gives us the same thing the other way round. In the first part of it he showed us Jesus teaching new truths about the scope of his kingdom in a dispute with the Pharisees. Here we see him translating his sermon into action and showing himself as good as his word.

In his sermon he had set aside the restrictive traditions of the Pharisees and opened a door into all the world. Now he himself goes through the door to begin a journey among the Gentiles. It was an extensive circular tour. For to go from Galilee to Tyre and Sidon (24) and then back through the middle of Decapolis (31) was something like going from Dumfries to Glasgow and Stirling and then back by the Scott country, or from Brussels to Rotterdam and the Hague, and back through the middle of the Ruhr. It looks rather like a symbolic journey into Gentile country. And it is certainly plain that here too, as everywhere, he comes to bring healing and help. Indeed the only thing Mark tells us from the whole tour is the story of two healings, one at least of which is quite unmistakably the healing of a Gentile. Mark is most emphatic about that, for he underlines it three times: he says it was done in the neighbourhood of Tyre and Sidon, which was Gentile country, he tells us it was done for a Greek-speaker of Syrophoenician birth, and he recalls how Jesus referred to her as a 'dog'—which in these days meant a Gentile as surely as 'nigger' now means a negro or 'chink' a Chinaman. That all goes to show once again how literally Jesus carries out in action the promises of his sermons. So often we say it is not words that count, but deeds. Well, here we have it also in deeds—the promise that his kingdom and its blessings are not only for the Jews, but also for the Gentiles. The idea is not so revolutionary now as it was then. Christ's claims and his gifts are not only for the West, but equally also for the East, not only for the white people, or the clever people, or even the good people, but for us all without exception. We have got used to that—as an idea. And yet if we believed it not only with the top of our minds but from the bottom of our hearts—if we not only accepted it but also practised it—then the effect on our lives would be pretty revolutionary still.

But to come back again for a moment to Jesus and the Pharisees. In his sermon Jesus had said their religion of separation was wrong, because God will not be served at the expense of our fellow men but can only be served in full fellowship with them. He had also said separation was useless, because no outward separation can remedy the real source of pollution, which is within. And he had made it plain that his new order was to bring men inward cleansing and new fellowship with each other. Now we see that actually happening in the two miracles Mark singles out here. In one Jesus cures a girl with an 'unclean spirit'—and whatever we have to understand by that, at all events it is obviously an inward sickness, a disorder of the soul, or spirit, or 'heart'. In the other he removes an obvious impediment to fellowship—for who is more obviously cut off from his fellow men than a man who can neither hear nor speak? He could hardly have given a more striking practical demonstration that he is wholly in earnest about what he says—that he does not merely mean to *talk* about the need for clean hearts and closer relations with our fellows, but is also able and willing to *do* whatever is necessary to create these things. Here is the answer to the question that must have arisen in our minds a moment ago. How can the idea that his claims and his blessings apply equally to us all get down through our minds into our hearts, so that we really believe it and our lives are moulded by it? How can all the many separations and divisions between us and our fellows be bridged, so that we can all respond together to his claims and together enjoy his blessings? The answer is, that it will be *his* doing. It will happen when *he* takes charge of our hearts and when *he* puts our relationships in order. And he will. He promised it then, and in Tyre and Decapolis he did it. He has promised the same to us, and he will do it still.

But is he able as well as willing? Is he able to deal not only with the comparatively simple problems of the first century, but also with the vastly more complicated troubles of our over-sophisticated hearts and our over-civilized society? Here there is another answer also to that. Jesus had taken the text of his sermon from a passage in Isaiah which proclaimed God's promise to redeem his people, and he had spoken in a way that made it almost obvious that he himself was the promised Redeemer. Now that, too, is doubly underlined in action. First Jesus tries to avoid publicity but 'cannot be hid' (24) because a Gentile woman recognizes him. And that recalls another of Isaiah's pictures of God's chosen Servant, who would 'not cry nor lift up nor cause his voice to be heard in the street', yet even without advertising himself would shine as a 'light to lighten the Gentiles' (Isa. 42.2, 6). Thus here we have still another practical sign that this Jesus is the chosen Servant and Redeemer. And if that is so, then he comes not merely with human resources but has behind him the whole power of God which is equal to any problem. And yet even that is not all, for as if to make assurance doubly sure Mark goes on to direct our attention to what happened after the second miracle. Then the people acclaimed Jesus with the words, 'He hath done all things well: he maketh both the deaf to hear and the dumb to speak' (37). Now, according to another of Isaiah's promises, it was God himself who would 'make the deaf to hear and the dumb to speak' (Isa. 35.4 f). And the words, 'He hath done all things well' come straight from the first chapter of Genesis—slightly different in our English translation, but identical in the Greek Bible—and it was none other than God the Creator who 'made all things well' (Gen. 1.31). Like as not these people did not realize what they were doing. But surely Mark, with his fine sense of dramatic irony, means *us* to recognize it: consciously or unconsciously they were hailing Jesus as the promised Redeemer and Bringer of the New Creation.

Yet Mark has more to do here than show Jesus practising what he preached. This passage does not only tell how he himself went through the door his words had opened to the Gentiles, how he followed up what he had said about the need for clean hearts and for fellowship by himself giving spiritual cleansing and removing obvious obstacles to fellowship, how he fulfilled the prophets in deed as well as in word and was acclaimed as the promised Redeemer who creates his world anew. These verses have also at least three other things to tell us about him.

For one thing, they make it clear again that he is our *Lord*. We have no claims on him, and though his mercy is not inexorable we have no kind of right to it. We can only hold out empty hands and beg and keep on begging. That is the point of the strange conversation here between Jesus and the woman. Jews might have tried to argue that for all their disobedience, God's own promises still entitled them to be treated as his children. But this Gentile woman had not even an argument like that to stand on. Compared to the Jews, Jesus said, she was not a child but merely a dog, and could not expect to be cared for at the children's expense. To that she answered, 'Yes, Lord: yet the dogs under the table eat of the children's crumbs' (28). And that is what moved him to grant her request after all: 'For this saying go thy way; the devil is gone out of thy daughter' (29). What was it about her answer that so appealed to him? Hardly just her smartness in turning his words to her own advantage. That might well have won over a harder heart than his. But surely what moved him far more was the one little word 'Lord', and the fact that it was obviously not just a polite form of address but meant seriously—seriously enough to accept whatever he liked to say of her and still not be put off. Let him compare her to a dog. Very well, she would not take offence but would behave like a dog—and not a petted lapdog either, but a hungry mongrel begging for scraps. She was ready to submit humbly to his judgment and to persevere with her prayer.

Is it because we are not prepared to do that that so many of our prayers go unanswered? We turn to him in trouble and ask for help. But if he then behaves as our Lord instead of our servant, if he should say hard things of us instead of doing what we want, then we are offended and go off to sulk. A man once declared he had left the Anglican Church because he was required to repeat in the General Confession at every service, 'We have erred and strayed like lost sheep', and he refused to be likened to a sheep. There was another who objected to being called a 'miserable sinner' because he felt neither wicked nor miserable—he had his faults and his disappointments like everyone else, but on the whole he was a very good chap and quite happy about it. No doubt there is something rather ludicrous about these two examples. But they come near enough the bone to be uncomfortable as well as ludicrous. We have got so used to thinking well of ourselves that we resent the many offensive things the Bible says about us. We have talked so long about the 'rights of man' that we now imagine God is as much bound by them as any. The result is, there is something argumentative about much of our praying, even something imperious as if we were somehow entitled to a favourable answer. Yet what is the sense of calling him 'Lord, Lord' and then expecting him to do the things *we* say? It is not surprising if he should appear to refuse that kind of asking. But perhaps he is only testing out how deep our acknowledgment of his Lordship goes. Perhaps he is only waiting for us to come off our high horse and humbly accept his judgment of us—as dogs, sheep, miserable sinners, 'utterly made opposite to all good', or whatever it may be. The woman in the story, at any rate, stood the test. Whatever happened, she would continue to bow before her Lord with empty hands, relying solely on his undeserved mercy. The person who is willing to do that is the person least likely to go away with hands still empty.

Another thing Mark shows us here is that Jesus is the Lord *whose word is enough*. He says to the woman, 'The devil is gone out of thy daughter' (29)—and so it was (30). He says to the deaf mute, 'Be opened' (34)—'and straightway his ears were opened, and the string of his tongue was loosed, and he spake plain' (35). The point is, that where this Lord speaks, things happen—whether we see the difference at once or not. The man knew immediately that he could hear and speak; the woman had to wait till she got home before she saw her daughter was really cured. Often as not we are like the woman and are left for a while to believe the truth of what we do not yet see. And often as not that does not suit us, but we want things the other way round. 'Seeing is believing', we say, 'I shall believe it when I see it.' But that is one of these glib sayings that sound fine but will not bear scrutiny. The fact is, that when we see a thing, then there is no longer any need to believe it at all. And the fact is, that most of the great blessings of one kind or another that have come man's way in the course of history have come through men who first believed what they did not yet see, and then worked for what they believed until they did see it. But however that may be, at all events to believe in Jesus as our Lord is to believe the truth of what he says, however long we may have to wait for the 'proof' of it. How typical was God's word to Moses of old: 'This shall be a token unto thee that I have sent thee: when thou hast brought forth the people out of Egypt, ye shall serve God on this mountain' (Ex. 3.12). The proof you shall have afterwards, when you reach the end of the journey. But already it is true, and you can set out believing the truth of it. That is how it is so often also with Jesus.

And the last thing Mark brings out here is that he is *our* Lord, right in our midst and identified most intimately with us. That seems to be the point of the rather curious details of the deaf mute's cure: 'He took him aside from the multitude, and put his fingers into his ears, and he spit, and touched his tongue; and looking up to heaven, he sighed, and saith unto him, Ephphatha, that is, Be opened' (33-34). It reads rather like some kind of primitive hocus-pocus that would be more in place in the realm of spells and incantations, and one wonders how it got into the Gospel, and why it was not enough for Jesus merely to speak his sovereign command as he did so often elsewhere. Or was this a kind of sign-language designed to communicate that command to a man to whom the ordinary spoken word meant nothing? The puzzle remains. But the very details that puzzle us serve also to mark our Lord's identification of himself with the sufferer in closest physical unity and deepest sympathy. It is as though he were offering his own good ears for the man's bad ears, giving his own sound tongue for the man's useless one. It is as if the healing virtue were literally to flow direct from his ears and tongue to the sufferer's, as the blood flows in a transfusion or the breath does in the 'kiss of life'.

And so the whole thing is a profound illustration of his dealings with all of us. Here he has brought us also apart like the deaf mute —even though we have no more claim on him than the Gentile woman. Here he offers us at his Table the visible sign and seal of the giving of his perfect life for the corrupt lives of us all: 'This is my body . . ., this is my blood . . .'. Here as we receive them he speaks his 'ephphatha' once more: be opened, deaf ears, to hear his word—be opened, dumb lips, to speak his praise—be opened, dull hearts, to receive his cleansing and to share and reflect his love. . . . Surely that makes a real difference. Surely we can *believe* it makes a difference, even if we do not yet see the change. Surely in that faith we can find a new openness both towards God and towards those around us.